Aging Gracefully with the Graces of Healing Prayer

William L. De Arteaga

with

Susan Brooks Thomas

EMETH PRESS
www.emethpress.com

Aging Gracefully with the Graces of Healing Prayer

Copyright © 2019 William L. De Arteaga

Printed in the United States of America on acid-free paper

All Scripture quotations, unless otherwise indicated, are taken from the Holy Bible, New International Version®, NIV®. Copyright ©1973, 1978, 1984, 2011 by Biblica, Inc.™ Used by permission of Zondervan. All rights reserved worldwide. www.zondervan.com The "NIV" and "New International Version" are trademarks registered in the United States Patent and Trademark Office by Biblica, Inc.™

ISBN 978-1-60947-149-1

Table of Contents

Introduction

Fifteen years ago, my wife Carolyn's primary physician saw some lab results that indicated her kidneys were having problems. The doctor sent Carolyn to the kidney specialist. He did another battery of tests and came back with the diagnosis that her kidneys were indeed failing. The prognosis was that in perhaps six months or a few years at most, she would have to go into a dialysis routine. The doctor ordered Carolyn to follow a low sodium diet, and warned that kidneys do not heal.

I am the cook of the house, and immediately converted to cooking without any added salt, using Dash and other spices instead of salt, and avoiding most processed foods, etc. More importantly, we immediately began healing prayers for her kidneys. For several Sundays at our church various intercessors would pray for her kidneys with the laying on of hands. We also prayed for Carolyn's healing in our home group in the form of a "holy huddle," where five or more of us would lay hands on her at the same time and agree for the healing of her kidneys.

As her husband I had a nightly prayer routine. I did the "pelvis thing" on Carolyn. This is a form of prayer whereby I would place my fingers lightly at the place where the pelvis bone is closest to the skin and speak healing to the kidneys. This type of prayer, developed by the husband and wife team, Charles and Frances Hunter, will be described below in detail. For now, let me just say that this prayer allows the healing energies of God to enter the lower torso area easily and do their healing work. After this, when we cuddled up in bed, I would place my hand on her kidney area and command healing to the kidneys and fall asleep with my hand on that area of the body. Sometimes I would feel a flow of energy (a slight tingling) in my hand. Francis MacNutt, the dean of Christian healing prayer, calls this type of prayer, where hands are laid on the person for an extended length of time, "soaking prayer."

Six months after her kidney diagnosis she returned to the same doctor for a check-up. Her kidneys had shown ***much improvement***. He was surprised, as the normal "best" result is stabilization of the kidney functions. She explained to the doctor, "We pray together for my healing every day." He said, "Hum, yes, prayer is good. I will recommend it to my other patients."[1] Carolyn has continued her yearly checkups, and a few years ago the indicators were going down again to a dangerous level – we had slacked off on prayer. So we caught up on our prayer routine, and her numbers came back up. The important thing is to note the difference between the hardships of dialysis, and living with a low sodium diet (which is actually no real bother). Prayer made the difference.

At a conference we attended later at Christian Healing Ministries in Jacksonville, Florida, Dr. Francis MacNutt spoke about healing and aging. He is among the most distinguished figures of the Christian healing renewal, and is now over 90 years old. (He is a World War II Navy veteran).[2] He observed that it is difficult to pray for the healing of certain age related illnesses or conditions. Thus for instance, it is usually not effective to pray over a bald man in his 60s and expect his hair to grow back as if he were in his 20s. It seems that we are designed to run down in the body even as we continue to grow spiritually. As Paul explained:

> Therefore, we do not lose heart. Though outwardly we are wasting away, yet inwardly we are being renewed day by day. For our light and momentary troubles are achieving for us an eternal glory that far outweighs them all. (2 Cor 4:15-17).

In short, prayer cannot nullify aging. But on the other hand it can make aging a gentle process, with much less pain, discomfort and medications

---

[1] See a fuller account of this in my wife's book, Carolyn Koontz De Arteaga, *Watching God Work: The Stuff of Miracles* (Alachua: Bridge-Logos, 2013) 42-43.

[2] MacNutt was the guiding person of the early Catholic Charismatic movement and learned healing prayer at the hand of Agnes Sanford. I detail this in my work, *Agnes Sanford and Her Companions* (Eugene: Wipf & Stock, 2015) chapter 20.

than normal. I became vividly aware of the latter in a check-up at the VA several years ago. I noticed men my age and younger go off with bags-full of prescriptions for high blood pressure, diabetes, etc. At seventy-three I had two prescriptions that helped control my enlarged prostate – that's all.

Healing prayer enables the Christian to transit into "elders" of ministry with grace and ease, as in my case, from a busy pastor, which is exhausting work, to writer and conference speaker where I can set my own pace.

Yours truly on the job as an OSL (Order of St Luke) speaker.
The OSL seeks to extend the knowledge of healing prayer
to all churches.

Healing prayer can mitigate the negative effects of aging, but not completely rejuvenate a person. This is due to the fact that Christians live in the Kingdom of God in the present age, and as theologians say, it is "Now, but not yet." That is, the portion of the Kingdom of God we have on earth is partial, and can be very effective, but it is not complete – not until the Second Coming. Then we will be perfectly healed and in brand new, ageless bodies.

1

Learning About Effective Healing Together

Learning of the Energies of God in the healing ministry

In the mid-1970s I first encountered the Christian healing ministry through the inner healing books of Ruth Carter Stapleton. The message of the books was very Christ-centered, and Mrs. Stapleton wrote in a clear and simple manner. She was also the brother of President Jimmy Carter. All this, plus the fact that inner healing was a new and exciting type of ministry, made her books best sellers.[1]

Inner healing encompasses various ways of praying for the negative memories that afflict a person and often result in neurotic or destructive behavior. In inner healing prayer (discussed below) the memories are neutralized with the invited presence of the Lord in the hurtful memories, and this prayer most often has lasting healing/behavioral results.[2]

---

[1] Stapleton, Ruth Carter. *The Gift of Inner Healing* (Waco: Word, 1976). And *The Experience of Inner Healing* (Waco: Word, 1977). Her books are charming, but theologically simplistic. This led later on to problems which had to be corrected by the classic work on inner healing, John Sandford's, *The Transformation of the Inner Man*. (South Plainfield: Bridge, 1982).

[2] For a description of how inner healing was discovered and developed see my work, *Agnes Sanford* chapter 17, "Harry and the Healing of Memories."

It turns out that Mrs. Carter Stapleton had learned inner healing from Agnes Sanford. I later discovered that this lady was one of the key figures of the Twentieth Century Christian healing revival.[3] Providentially, just as I heard about Agnes Sanford, my sister sent me a copy of Agnes Sanford's classic work, *The Healing Light.*[4] I was delighted by it as it clarified some things I had experienced, specifically the tingling or vibration sensations I and others often felt when we laid hands on someone for healing. Mrs. Sanford saw this was the body's sensing God's light and energy passing through us and into the supplicant's body. No one before had ever described healing in this "energy" way as clearly.

Dr. Francis MacNutt, then a Dominican priest, took Mrs. Sanford's understanding and developed a teaching on "soaking prayer" from it. That is, he advocated the extended and patient laying on of hands on the supplicant for healing.

I recall vividly one conference Carolyn and I attended, about 1982. Fr. McNutt invited an elderly woman to the front. She was suffering from fluid in her knees that made them enlarged and painful for her to walk. He assigned a healing team of three persons to pray for her healing with the laying on of hands directly on the afflicted area. The intercessory team continued to pray for the woman while McNutt resumed his talk. When he had finished, about a half hour later, he turned to the team for a progress report. Indeed, the swelling had noticeably receded, and the nun could walk with much agility and no pain, although some swelling remained. Carolyn and I were much impressed at this public demonstration of soaking prayer, and we have continued to use it in our ministry together and on ourselves, as the situation warrants.

But let me clarify the issue of the energies of God. There is a large gap in western Christian theology, both Catholic and Protestant, about the energies of God. These energies are often confused with the person of the Holy Spirit, or with the concept of grace. In fact, there was no theology of the energies of God in western Christianity until the advent of Mrs.

---

[3] I make the point, and I believe it is not an exaggeration that Agnes Sanford was the greatest original theologian of the 20th Century.

[4] Agnes Sanford, *The Healing Light* (St. Paul: MacAlester Park, 1947).

Agnes Sanford's *The Healing Light* in 1947.[5] But because Mrs. Sanford's work was devotional, i.e. on the healing ministry, and not "serious theology," her insights into the energies of God were ignored by Christian theologians. In those decades they were mostly occupied with the project of explaining away the miracles in Scripture as unnecessary mythology – mistakenly called "higher criticism.".

Before we go further, we need to go to several scriptures which point to the energies of God as distinct from the personhood of the Holy Spirit. A key passage comes from a scene described by the prophet Ezekiel about the reformed Temple service, specifically at the moment the priests come out of the sanctuary from offering sacrifice.

> When they go out into the outer court, into the outer court to the people, they shall put off their garments in which they have been ministering and lay them in the holy chambers; then they shall put on other garments so that they will not transmit holiness to the people with their garments. (Ezek. 44:19-20)

The issue here is that the priests' garments were full of the energies of God. It is unexplained why the "people" should not touch it. The people at this period in history had scant access to the word of God directly, and had it read to them only on special occasions. Thus, they would be unprepared for a spiritual blessing. I am reminded of analogous situations in my journey in the Charismatic Renewal in which I saw immature Christians receive the Baptism of the Spirit. They then used their gifting in boastful or inappropriate ways, as in blurting out prophetic utterances that were mixed with "fleshy" thoughts. Paul warned us not to lay hands on someone hastily (1 Tim 5:22), which I believe means don't transmit to him or her an anointing before he or she is ready. It seems this is the meaning of the Ezekiel passage cited above.

Another point in the Ezekiel scripture is that the energies of God are, as Agnes Sanford pointed out in *The Healing Light*, similar to electrical energy, which can cook your breakfast and make your toast, or give you a nasty shock if you touch a live wire.

---

[5] Ibid.

In the New Testament we don't directly see such a mistake, and only have Paul's warning to Timothy on this. Rather, the energies of God do good, as in Jesus' garment which was touched by the woman with the issue of blood (Luke 8: 43-48). The Gospel account is particularly clear in that "power," *dynamin*, left Jesus' garment to do the healing work. That is energy at work. The Western theological tradition has been so deficient on this that the King James Bible translated this passage with the word "virtue" for *dynamin* - a translation atrocity.

Even in modern times translators have tended to downplay the word energy. For instance, the translation of the NAS Bible, which is known for its literalness, translates Colossians 1:29 in this way: "For this purpose also I labor, striving according to His power, which mightily works within me." The word "power" in Greek is *energia* and should have been translated as "energy."

Note also, we are informed in the book of Acts that Paul's aprons and handkerchiefs were carried to the sick and demon possessed, and they were healed by contact with these items, just as Jesus' clothing was energized. (Acts 19:11-13).

There is another scripture, in the Old Testament, puzzling to many commentators, but is understandable if one reads it as dealing with the energies of God. It is the incident of the resuscitation from the dead of the Shunamite woman's son (2 Kings 4). In that incident the woman came to Elisha, and before she spoke the prophet discerned that the boy was dead:

> Elisha said to Gehazi, [his disciple] "Tuck your cloak into your belt, take my staff in your hand and run. Don't greet anyone you meet, and if anyone greets you, do not answer. Lay my staff on the boy's face." But the child's mother said, "As surely as the LORD lives and as you live, I will not leave you." So he got up and followed her. Gehazi went on ahead and laid the staff on the boy's face, but there was no sound or response. So Gehazi went back to meet Elisha and told him, "The boy has not awakened." When Elisha reached the house, there was the boy lying dead on his couch. He went in, shut the door on the two of them and prayed to the LORD. Then he got on the bed and lay on the boy, mouth to mouth, eyes to eyes, hands to hands. As he stretched himself out on him, the boy's body grew warm. Elisha turned away and walked back and forth in the room and then got on the

bed and stretched out on him once more. The boy sneezed seven times and opened his eyes. (NIV vs. 29-35)

Why this strange action about Elisha's staff? Why would Gehazi inform Elisha that the "boy has not awakened"? It is understandable if we see that Elisha's staff had, through continuous contact with the great prophet, an endowment of the energies of God, and that Elisha believed that energy would possibly be enough to resuscitate the boy. It did not, so he did "plan B" to bring the boy back. He laid on him directly so that the energies of God in his body and clothing would complete the job. St. Paul would use Elisha's method of resuscitation (body to body) when the young man Eutycus fell to his death (Acts 20:8-10).

To understand the theological gap about the energies of God, we need to know something of Early Church history. The overwhelming majority of Early Church theologians (the "Church Fathers") followed and adhered to the philosophical system of Plato. This is especially true of St. Augustine of Hippo (354-430 A.D.), whose theology laid the foundations of Catholic theology and much inspired John Calvin and his Reformed Protestantism. Plato's philosophy centered on things that were permanent, as in his famous and imaginary "forms," but paid little attention to temporary things such as energy, which comes and goes. Aristotle, whose philosophy later became the basis of St. Thomas Aquinas' theology (and became the official theology of Roman Catholicism), also had a prejudice for the permanent vs. the temporary. His philosophy favored "essences" which were permanent, as against "accidental" characteristics which were temporary. The transitory nature of energy was not a focus of either Plato's or Aristotle's philosophical system.[6] Thus, classical Western theology, based on the

---

[6] I learned of this problem in classic Greek Philosophy from Karl R. Popper's now classic work, *The Open Society and its Enemies* (London: G. Routledge & Sons, 1947) in which he traces the West's totalitarian ideologies to Plato and Hegel. See especially vol. 1, "The spell of Plato." In print in various later editions. Had the philosophies of the pre-Socratics been in vogue at the time of the Father's seminal writings, more attention might have been given to energy as a major concern and focus. What would a Heraclitus based Christian theology look like?

Fathers, never gave sufficient attention to the "energies of God," either in their scriptural examples, or their theological implications.

Eastern Orthodoxy and the energies of God

It is somewhat a different story in Eastern Orthodoxy. There, the monastic tradition of intense prayer made the monks aware of the light of God as a real phenomenon. This was elaborated in the theological writings of St. Symeon the "New Theologian" (945-1022 A.D.), one of the most important theologians of Eastern Orthodoxy. St. Symeon had various mystical experiences in which he was enraptured in the light, love and energies of God. He went on to develop a theology of this. He believed, and Eastern orthodoxy had followed him here, that God in his essence is unknowable, but He chooses to make himself known to us through his "uncreated energies." These energies permeate the entire universe but are intensified and shown to the Christian during prayer.[7]

"Falling under the power" as the energies of God in action

Observers have recorded the "fallings" in practically every major revival. That is, a person temporarily losing control of their nervous system and falling to the floor. They have recorded that a person who "falls" often come up healed or transformed. For instance, the Rev. John Lyle, a Presbyterian minister and participant in the famous Cane Ridge revival of 1801, (the start of the Second Great Awakening) wrote in his diary:

> ...we began to talk and pray for those that were fallen down and -------- a deist fell, son to widow ------. ... He had said just before he would not fall

---

[7] There several new studies on St. Symeon, as well as translations and studies of his works. See *Symeon the New Theologian*, Trans. By C.T. Catanzaro (New York: Paulist Press, 1980). A difficult but insightful article by: Pachomios Penkett, "Symeon the New Theologian's vision of the Godhead," *Phronema*, 15 (2000), 97-114. And especially useful: Vladimir Lossky, *The Mystical Theology of the Eastern Church* (Crestwood; St. Valimir's Seminary Press, 1976), Chapter 4 "Uncreated Energies." St. Symeon and Agnes Sanford's views on the energies of God coincide to an amazing degree - an excellent topic for a scholarly paper or dissertation for someone out there.

so for a thousand dollars and that he did not believe in heaven, hell of the devil. Shortly after two of his cousins fell. He lay speechless for an hour or two then spoke and said he had been ridiculing the work before he fell and said he wanted to seek Christ.[8]

A.J Tomlinson, one of the most important figures of Early Pentecostalism and eventually an overseer of the Church of God, had a similar experience with the energies of God after a lengthy time of praying for the Baptism of the Holy Spirit. As he approached the altar at a revival service:

> "My mind was clear, but a peculiar power so enveloped and thrilled my whole being that I concluded to yield myself up to God and await results. . . As I lay there great joy flooded my soul. The happiest moments I had ever known up to that time. I never knew what real joy was before. ... Oh, such floods and billows of glory ran through my whole being for several minutes!"

He arose speaking in tongues.[9]

Now, let me connect the dots on what happens in a Pentecostal or charismatic "healing line" when someone "falls under the power," or as Dr. MacNutt calls it, "rests in the Spirit,"[10] using my wife's example. Carolyn was born an underweight baby, and in addition her mother almost died giving her birth. Carolyn was placed in an incubator and not expected to live, and her father focused on attending to his wife in the first critical days. This event "imprinted" deeply in her memory. In her life Carolyn often felt fears of abandonment for trivial reasons. For instance, one Saturday I left early in the morning while she was asleep to go to a men's church breakfast. When she awoke she thought I had left her for good and experienced tremendous anxiety (she forgot I told her about the breakfast the day before).

Sometime later Carolyn "rested in the Spirit" during a healing line, and during her "carpet time" had a vision of Jesus smiling at her and loving her

---

[8] Catherine C. Cleveland, *The Great Revival in the West, 1797-1805* (Chicago: The University of Chicago Press, 1916), 187.

[9] A. J. Tomlinson, *The Last Great Conflict* (Cleveland: Press of Walter Rogers, 1913) 211-212.

[10] Francis MacNutt, *Overcome by the Spirit*. (Terrytown: Chosen, 1990).

as a baby in the incubator. This was a great healing to her, and she has not suffered from separation anxiety since.

I believe what happened to her was that when the healing evangelist touched her forehead a jolt of the ***energies of God*** went into her which temporarily immobilized her neurological system and she fell down. At that point the Holy Spirit ministered to her in the vision she experienced. The falling was because of the energies of God - the vision was the work of the person of the Holy Spirit to give healing to her soul and glory to Jesus.[11]

Learning about command healing

In 1986 Carolyn and I ran into persons who were praying for the sick in what seemed to be an unusual manner – by command. They would say things like, "In Jesus' name, I command the spirit of arthritis out, and normality to be restored to this knee."[12] It seemed to us as something only Jesus or an Apostle could do. This command mode is different from the petition mode which is normative to most contemporary Christians. For instance, "Father, in Jesus' name, please heal this arthritic knee." Petition prayers for healing are found in the Psalms and other sections of the Old Testament, and are certainly valid and effective. But they are not found in the New Testament for any form of healing or deliverance situation.

We were introduced to the command form of prayer when we were invited to attend a healing course taught by a saintly elderly couple, Zeb and Maida Burnett (both have gone to be with the Lord). They taught from the materials developed by Charles and Frances Hunter, a Pentecostal couple who brought command healing to world-wide attention (more on them below).

---

[11] I develop the theme of the energies of God more fully in my blog posting: "The "Energies of God" From the "Fallings" to the "Jerusalem Syndrome,'" *Anglican Pentecostal*. Posted Nov. 8, 2013.   https://anglicalpentecostal.blogspot.com/2013/11/energies-of-god-from-fallings-to.html

[12] This chapter is based on my earlier blog posting, "The Hunter's Revolution in Healing Ministry," *The Anglican Pentecostal*. Posted May 8, 2013. http://anglicalpentecostal.blogspot.com/2013/05/the-hunters-revolution-in-healing.html

When we came to the course Carolyn and I had already learned much about healing prayer from classic Pentecostal and charismatic teachers, such as Derik Prince, Mrs. Agnes Sanford, Fr. Frances MacNutt, and others, both at their conferences, and through their books and tapes. We were grateful for all of these, and especially for MacNutt's teaching on soaking prayer, but we became convinced the Hunter insights were both soundly biblical and often more effective than the traditional petition prayers that had been modeled for us.

Before going further, let me briefly cite the New Testament scriptures on this, because it is still unfamiliar to many Christians. Command healing was apparently done by the disciples from their first commissioning when Jesus sent them into the countryside of Judea: "The seventy-two returned with joy and said, "Lord, even the demons submit to us in your name." (Luke 10:17) Although we have no descriptions of exactly how the seventy-two ministered to the sick and demon possessed, it is significant that they were amazed by their *authority*. They said nothing about the elegance of their prayers, etc. So whatever they said to chase out the demons rested on their authority as disciples of Jesus and the use of his name.

From earliest times Christians have practiced the exorcism/deliverance of evil spirits as a direct command to the malignant entities, but past Apostolic times commands for healing were not used regularly. This is particularly unfortunate because all the accounts of healings recorded in Acts were ministered through commands. For example, when Peters saw the lame beggar near the Temple:

> Then Peter said, "Silver or gold I do not have, but what I have I give you. In the name of Jesus Christ of Nazareth, walk." Taking him by the right hand, he helped him up, and instantly the man's feet and ankles became strong. (Acts 3: 6-7)

Command healing in Jesus' name was not just a prerogative of the Apostles, as some commentators claim. We see the command healing mode described in Paul's retelling of his healing from the blindness he suffered when he first met the risen Lord on the road to Damascus.

> "A man named Ananias came to see me. He was a devout observer of the

law and highly respected by all the Jews living there. He stood beside me and said, `Brother Saul, receive your sight!' And at that very moment I was able to see him." (Acts 22:12-13)

Note the command mode. How and why the post-Apostolic Christians drifted into healing via petition prayer has not been examined, but it certainly must be understood as part of the general decline of the healing ministry that took place from the Third Century on. Christians in modern times who have believed in healing prayer have almost universally prayed prayers of petition for healing. This is partly because prayers of petition are an important and valid way to pray, as for instance, for a new job, and we are most accustomed to it. But to repeat, it is *not* the New Testament pattern for healing prayer (or exorcism).

But now let me say a few things about the Hunters themselves.[13] Charles (1920 - 2010) and Frances (1916 - 2009) were a graced and humble couple. In spite of the large revenues generated by their books and tapes, they collected only a modest salary from their ministry organization (the Billy Graham pattern). They donated the rest of their royalties back into their healing and evangelism ministry. Scandal never touched their ministry.

Charles and Frances met and married late in their lives, in 1970. Charles had been a believer all of his life, but in a cessationist denomination, which believed that healing and the gifts of the Spirit ceased after the Apostles died. However, he and his first wife, Jeanne, had read Agnes Sanford's *Healing Light* and Genevieve Parkhurst's *Healing and Wholeness Are Yours.*[14] Mrs. Parhurst was a disciple of Mrs. Sanford, and with her helped develop the inner healing ministry. Through those books Charles and Jeanne had come to reject cessationism and to believe in healing prayer for this day.

---

[13] Other than *Charisma* magazine, the Christian press has ignored the Hunters. A Google search gives their website and where to buy their books, plus some ignorant anti-cult sites – the web is full of them. A search in the Christian academic literature shows no hits. The *Charisma* articles are: Bill Shepson's, "Still Happy After All These Years," *Charisma* (August 2000) 95, and E.S Caldwell's, "It is the Hour to Believe," *Charisma & Christian Life*, (October, 1987).

[14] Sanford, *Healing Light*, and Genevieve Parkhurst, *Healing and Wholeness Are Yours* (St. Paul: Macalester Park, 1957).

Mrs. Jeanne Hunter came down with ovarian cancer, and in seeking prayer support for her healing, Charles contacted Mrs. Parkhurst. She came to visit and to pray with Jeanne. The hospital room where Jeanne lay seemed filled with the glory of God, and Jeanne rallied. During this period, she received a deep inner healing. But ultimately she passed away, happy to go to her Lord. ("Now, but not yet").[15] Charles grieved his wife's loss, but he knew that she had gone to her true home, and renewed his own ministry of evangelization.

Frances had been a widow for many years, and became a born-again Christian when she was forty-nine. At that point she became a self-described "Gospel fanatic" and joined an Evangelical church. She learned soul-winning through Campus Crusade for Christ. Frances discovered she had a special anointing in this and practiced it whenever and however she could. She wrote about her efforts in her first book, *God is Fabulous.*[16]

She also learned about the Holy Spirit's gifts. Although her church was not charismatic or Pentecostal, Frances began reading some of the charismatic books then just coming to print. On one of her evangelistic tours to Houston, Frances was introduced by a local pastor to Charles Hunter, and within a few months they were married. Soon after, they began ministering together. But now, not only proclaiming salvation, but the message of Pentecost and healing.

From the very start of their ministry the Hunters observed and learned healing techniques from a multitude of sources. They picked up the long-standing Pentecostal technique of praying for a person's backache by "leg extension." That is, having the person sit in a chair and praying that the legs be equalized in length. As the legs equalize the spinal column comes into alignment and often this heals the backache.

---

[15] The story of her sickness and death is told in Charles Hunter's, *A Tribute to God* (Kingswood: Hunter Ministries, 2008) Mrs. Parkhurst's ministry to Jeanne is found on pp. 17-43.

[16] Frances Gardner Hunter, *God is Fabulous: The Story of an "Unsaved Christian"* (New York: Family Library, 1973).

Yours truly giving instruction on the "leg extension"
at a healing mission.
Photo was taken by author's wife and is in our possession.

They learned a similar technique, arm extension, from healing evangelist, Joe Poppell. He had been doing it for years to heal upper back pain and chest disorders.

As the Hunters ministered they experienced many miraculous healings. But not to the degree that they expected and saw described in the Bible, where all who came to Jesus were healed. (Matt 8:16).[17] They asked the Lord for a breakthrough. The Lord told them to study Acts carefully. Charles described what happened:

One night a man came on the stage, held up by two people, and leaning heavily on two walking canes. He did not have the strength to lift his feet off the floor; he scooted them along. When we finished praying, instead of saying "Praise the Lord and go on your way," we said, "PICK UP YOUR

---

[17] It should be noted that in Jesus' own hometown, Nazareth, his healing powers were limited by lack of faith in the population (Matt 13:58).

CANES AND WALK!" He lifted his canes off the floor and slid his feet forward, and he didn't fall! Pretty soon I was running alongside of him across the stage, and he began to say, "Praise the Lord!"[18]

Now, what makes this moment significant is not that it was an original discovery, which it was not. Such commands have been recorded in the lives of the saints and heroes of the Church.[19] For example, spoken healing commands were common in the ministry of the famous faith teacher and healer, Smith Wigglesworth (1859-1947). In one of his several resuscitations from the dead he came into a sick room as a woman died:

> ...I reached over into the bed and pulled her out. I carried her across the room, stood her against the wall and held her up, as she was absolutely dead. I looked into her face and said, "In the name of Jesus I rebuke this death." Her whole body began to tremble. "In the name of Jesus, I command you to walk," I said. I repeated, "In the name of Jesus, walk!" and she walked.[20]

The Hunters great innovation and gift to Christendom was that thereafter they did it consistently, and taught command healing as the *prerogative of every believer*. It was not just those especially gifted with faith such as Smith Wigglesworth.

At the beginning they believed that it was necessary to *shout* healing commands. My sister, a Catholic nun, and who was among the first in her religious order to become a charismatic, recalls a healing event that the Hunter's did in her parish in Scarsdale, New York (about 1975). A large Catholic charismatic group came, over four hundred people, and although some healings were done, most person were entirely put off by the Hunter's shouts and commands. The Hunters soon discerned that the authority of the command did not depend on its decibel level.

---

[18] Charles Hunter, and Frances Hunter, *How to Heal the Sick,* (Kingwood: Hunter Ministries, 1981) 45-46.

[19] Agnes Sanford in her classic work, *The Healing Light* (1947) gave an example of command healing in her own life, but does not make it a major point, and can be easily missed, p.77.

[20] Stanley Howard Frodsham, *Smith Wigglesworth: Apostle of Faith,* (Springfield: Gospel Publishing House, 1990) 59. Originally published in 1948.

In spite of this and other missteps, the Hunters learned quickly and adjusted. For instance, in order to focus the force of the command (and healing energies), they began asking the supplicant, "What does the doctor say about your situation?" This proved to be very helpful in understanding exactly what was wrong and what organ was afflicted. Through trial and error, and consultation with medical professionals, they developed patterns of command prayers for specific diseases. For example, in praying for a person with diabetes they would cast out any spirit of inheritance, then command a new pancreas to be formed "in the name of Jesus."[21]

In 1981 the Hunters published their now classic work, *How to Heal the Sick*. This book incorporated a quasi-chiropractic understanding of healing ministry. That is, they had learned from chiropractic physicians, and from observing the results of the arms and foot extensions, that straightening the spine and bringing it to normality was an effective part in healing all sorts of ailments. This is basic to chiropractic theory and practice. They added two other forms of the laying on of hands, one to the neck and another to the pelvis, which I used on my wife for her kidney problem (see introduction above). All of these were combined with commands for healing.

A renowned chiropractor, Dr. Roy Le Roy, heard about the Hunter's ministry and came to witness one of their events with the specific intention of exposing and debunking them. He was astounded at what he saw, and became instead their close friend and ministry adviser.[22] He produced videos and wrote a book to support the Hunter discoveries in healing.

We should make it clear, that the Hunter method and books *do not teach chiropractic manipulation*. Rather they teach the laying on of hands in conjunction with command prayer - and the Holy Spirit does the spine adjustments and other creative miracles.[23]

The Hunters were right about insisting that all Christians should lay hands on the sick. Their book, *If Charles and Frances Can Do It, You Can*

---

[21] Hunter, *Handbook of Healing,* (Kingswood: Hunter Books, 1983) 114.

[22] Dr. Roy J. Le Roy, and Norma Jean Le Roy, *The Supernatural Spine* (Kingwood: Hunter Books, 1993).

[23] For example, see the chiropractic charts in the Hunter's book, *If Charles and Frances Can Do It, You Can Do It!* (Kingswood: Hunter Publications, 1997), 44, 92-93.

Do It Too! says it again and again.[24] What they do not mention is that indeed there are persons with unusual gifts of healing, including themselves. Frances had, for instance, a special anointing to heal cancer – a difficult disease to tackle. Proclaiming that any Christian can minister healing prayer as well as they was an encouragement to others, but also an exaggeration. Few people have the level of faith and anointing they had.

But their effort to integrate new medical findings, chiropractic and otherwise, with specific prayers is noteworthy and something that Christians in the healing ministry should follow. In fact, one of the reasons for the great success of the Hunter's healing methods and career is that they have operated in the Biblically mandated mode of "testing discernment." Paul wrote to the Thessalonians: "Do not put out the Spirit's fire; do not treat prophecies with contempt. Test everything. Hold on to the good. Avoid every kind of evil." (1Thess 5:19-21)

Paul wrote with the assumption of the continuous presence and activity of the Holy Spirit in the Church - and also the continuous presence of harassment and confusion caused by demonic spirits.[25] The theology of cessationism was far into the future and probably unimaginable to him. But Paul made it clear that Christians needed the tool of discernment/testing to separate what is good and from the Holy Spirit, from what is fluff, false or destructive – either "flesh" or demonic. Although the context of Paul's directions in 1 Thess 5 is the prophetic ministry, it is plain that what Paul meant by "test everything" was precisely that, to test every kind of spiritual activity, phenomenon, or manner of spirituality.

With the arrival of heavily doctrinal Christianity, and later with cessationism, the mandate to test was rendered incomprehensible, and in effect became a "historic" passage like 1 Cor 12, to be filed away as interesting but with no present application. The traditional churches, Catholic, Protestant or Eastern or Oriental Orthodox, believed they had it totally right, doctrinally and in practice - so what was there to test?

---

[24] Ibid.

[25] James Kallas, *The Satanward View: A Study of Pauline Theology* (Philadelphia: Westminster Press, 1956), is especially good on this latter point.

The ministry of Charles and Frances Hunter has been a golden example of testing discernment. They rediscovered the power of "command healing" and compared it to the biblical text for verification. They tested the utility of combining chiropractic understanding as part of healing prayer and found that it gave good fruit, even though it was not specifically mentioned in the Bible.

The Hunter method, command healing with the chiropractic insights, special leg and arm extensions, etc., is quicker than petition healing, and often produces results that can be immediately felt by the supplicant. This is especially significant in ministering to nominal Christians and agnostics, who normally would be quick to dismiss healing prayer as "nice poetry" but ineffective, or as psychosomatic event. Also, many people who seem to be OK, actually walk around with back problems, from minor to serious. Using the Hunter method gives immediate and accountable healing to many of these back problems. These people are amazed by the immediate relief, and for many it may be the first time that they have received a recognizable healing from any Christian or church group. Also, if a rapid healing is done to an unbeliever, such healings are a portal to immediate evangelization and a "decision for Christ" may follow right there. The healing takes the place of the introductory tract or evangelical sermon.[26]

Carolyn and I began to use some of the Hunter arm and leg extensions and command prayers as part of the normal healing ministry that took place right after Holy Communion in our church. We taught some of it to the church's intercessors group. The rector, noticed it, but did not like it. He called me into his office and told me command healings were part of the folly of the new "name it, claim it heresy" of the "Tulsa folks" (i.e., the "Faith" ministers, Kenneth Hagin, Kenneth Copeland, etc.). He would not be swayed by the scriptures I showed him and forbade us to do it at his church.

That saddened me and I *tried* to be obedient. Wouldn't you know, a few Sundays later Carolyn and I were again on prayer team duty, and a person

---

[26] I stress these points in my book, *The Public Prayer Station: Taking Healing to the Streets and Evangelizing the Nones* (Lexington: Emeth, 2018).

came to us with a terrible backache – just the thing the Hunter method does best. I fudged, and healed the man via the "arm extension" – just as the rector glanced over at us. After several other incidents we left that church. We sought another church home and landed at St. Jude's of Marietta, a really great church, where we stayed for over a decade. The rector there, Fr. Frank Baltz, was Bible-believing and totally orthodox.[27] He had no problem with the Hunter method.

But even at St. Jude's we found resistance to the command mode of healing prayer (this was 1989). Fr. Baltz invited me to lead one of the home Bible study groups of the church. The host of the home found the Hunter method "presumptuous and offensive," and broke up the group rather than have us pray in that way at her home.

All of this happened decades ago. In recent years the command method of healing prayer has percolated through many churches and is more widely accepted, though some more conservative groups still oppose it as heresy, and the web is full of ignorant Christian anti cult sites that lambaste the Hunters and their teaching.

---

[27] His master's thesis at seminary was on Agnes Sanford. It stressed her link to the Anglican tradition of healing prayer. Baltz, Frances B. "Agnes Sanford: A Creative Intercessor." MA thesis, Nashotah House, 1979.

2

A Marriage Partnership
for Gracious Aging

But now let me share some more of the ways that prayer has softened and graced the aging processes for Carolyn and myself. We pray together every day and use healing prayer on ourselves at the very start of any disease or abnormality. Even before we married we prayed for each other regularly. When I first met Carolyn she suffered from regular bouts of severe headaches. After several times praying over her, including several times over the phone, and teaching her how to pray for herself, they stopped completely.[1]

Besides continuously praying for one another, supplements have also played a role in our "graceful aging." Let me deal with the supplements issue briefly. At the beginning of the Charismatic Renewal back in the 1960s and 1970s, many charismatic teachers were denouncing supplements and herbal shops as occult and things to be avoided. Yes, some herbal shops were (and are) associated with all sorts of New Age stuff. An herbal and supplements shop in my home town is one such place, filled with posters and advertisements of "Goddess" seminars, etc. But such broad brushing, unfortunately common in Christian circles, missed the point that God often uses unconventional folks to bring out some facet of truth ignored by traditional or establishment institutions. I have dealt with this issue in

---

[1] For a glimpse of our ministry together in healing, see Carolyn Koontz DeArteaga's, *Watching God Work.*

my books *Quenching the Spirit,* and *Agnes Sanford and Her Companions,* where I showed how Mary Baker Eddy's Christian Science shocked and shamed many churchmen to take a serious look at healing prayer as a present ministry for the Church. (When Christian Science arose in the 1880s healing prayer had been mostly forgotten in the orthodox churches).[2]

In any case, the herbal shops and health food "fanatics" of the 1960s and 1970s were harbingers of real and significant advances in how we achieve and maintain health.[3] From an informal inventory of my Christian friends now, fifty years later, I see most take some supplements daily. Some are members of Shaklee and other supplement companies.

The use of herbs and medication for health is actually clear in the Bible. Unfortunately, it is most clear in the "large Bible" – the canon of books used by the Catholics, Anglican, Oriental Orthodox and Eastern Orthodox Christians. Their canons contain books and sections of books written in Greek and not found in the Hebrew text of the Old Testament. These books, such as 1st and 2nd Maccabees, were in the Septuagint, the Hebrew Bible Jesus often quoted. But the Reformers did not include those Greek books in their translations of the printed Bible, so that today Protestants mostly disregard them.

One of these books, Ecclesiasticus, is especially important in reference to the healing ministry as it has a section which lauds doctors and medical herbs as gifts from God. The whole passage has tremendous wisdom:

> Treat the *doctor* with the *honor* that is his due, in consideration of his services; for he too has been created by the Lord. Healing itself comes from the Most High, like a gift received from a king. The doctor's learning keeps his head high, and the great regard him with awe. The *Lord* has brought forth medicinal herbs from the ground, and no one sensible *will* despise them. Did not a piece of wood once sweeten the water, thus giving *proof* of its power? He has also given some people knowledge, so that they may draw credit from his mighty works. He uses these for healing and relieving

---

[2] William De Arteaga, *Quenching the Spirit* (Lake Mary: Creation House, 1992. 1996) and *Agnes Sanford.*

[3] Actually, as early as the 1930, The Rev Robert B. H. Bell, and Episcopal priest, combined healing prayer and health foods into a Christian system for better health. See my *Agnes Sanford,* chapter 12.

pain; the druggist makes up a mixture from them. Thus, there is no end to his activities; thanks to him, well-being exists throughout the world. My child, when you are ill, do not rebel, but pray to the *Lord* and he *will* heal you. Renounce your faults, keep your hands unsoiled, and cleanse your heart from all sin. Offer *incense* and a memorial of fine flour, make as rich an offering as you can afford. Then let the *doctor* take over -- the *Lord* created him too -- do not let him leave you, for you need him. There are times when *good* health depends on doctors. For they, in their turn, *will* pray the *Lord* to grant them the *grace* to relieve and to heal, and so prolong your life. (Ecclesiasticus 38: 1-14)

Had Protestants valued this passage as inspired scripture many of the problems of the early Faith-Cure movement (1880s) and Pentecostalism (1900+) would have been avoided. Many of these early healing pioneers took a "faith vs medicine" stand. That is, if the Christians wanted God to heal his or her disease they had to renounce medication and rely solely on prayer for healing.[4] Echoes of this tragic mistake crop up every so often when some fundamentalist Christian denies medication such as insulin to his diabetic child. This causes scandal and heathens sneer at the ignorance of Christians.

Actually, there is a passage in the Old Testament that can be tweaked and expanded to mean the same thing. It is 2 Chr 16:2

In the thirty-ninth year of his reign Asa was afflicted with a disease in his feet. Though his disease was severe, even in his illness he did not seek help from the Lord, but only from the physicians.

Thus, trusting *some* in the work of physicians is OK as long as one also seeks the Lord. But this combination of medicine plus prayer it is certainly not as clear as the one we have cited from Ecclesiasticus.

In our household Carolyn became the main "health foods and supplement" person. This is reversal of role from when we first married. In 1970 I was the supplements guy and avid reader of *Prevention*, etc. With time I eased off, but have always taken some daily supplements. In the last de-

---

[4] I deal with this tragic misunderstanding and error in my work, *Quenching the Spirit*, chapter 6-7.

cade Carolyn's schedule permitted her to watch "The Doctor's" most days, and she kept me informed on new health food issues and discoveries, and, for instance, how dangerous belly fat is.

Doing the tourist thing in Chattanooga with my sister/sister on the left and Carolyn on the right. Sister Gloria has been a nun for over 60 years, and was one of the first in her order to embrace the Charismatic Renewal. She is on duty now as spiritual director in Guatemala. Why on earth would Carolyn worry about my belly fat?

But now to the main point, more on how prayer has eased our transition to old age. Carolyn's family was from Nova Scotia of Scotch descent, and apparently had a genetic tendency for macular degeneration. Her grandfather went totally blind by the time he was 50, as did one of her uncles. Carolyn was diagnosed ten years ago with eye problems at various stages, including the first signs of macular degeneration. From that point I prayed regularly for her eyes, command healing and the laying on of hands, and she began taking the Lutein based vitamin supplements just then discovered. When she went to the eye doctor for a checkup two years later he was surprised that it had not progressed at all. Prayer, and a few supplements, thank you Lord!

Fifteen years ago another eye specialist told her that she had an extremely thin retina, and that she would probably soon go blind, "In a few weeks, months, or at most few years."[5] He warned her to be especially careful not to fall, as that shock would certainly sever the thin retina. She came home shaken and I began laying hands on her eyes regularly and commanded healing for the retina to grow to normal thickness.

Carolyn was indeed especially careful not to fall. But oops! A few months after the bad news about her retina she stepped on the dog's food dish and fell on the hard ceramic kitchen floor with a thud. She opened her eyes expecting the worse, but nothing happened except a bruise on her thigh. She could see as well as before. In the next decade Carolyn fell several more times, once breaking her arm, and the last time breaking her femur bone. No loss of sight.

Carolyn went three years ago to an optometrist for a new pair of glasses.[6] It was a new person who gave her a complete examination. She told him about her thin retina, but as he looked at it carefully he said. "No, your retina is as good as most women your age. It must have been a misdiagnosis."[7] Funny how often we have heard that line. To this day she has not lost her sight, although she has cataracts that restrict her night vision and driving – "Now, but not yet." Again, the difference between total blindness and adequate vision comes from prayer – with a little assist from supplements.

---

[5] Story is told more fully in Koontz De Arteaga's, *Watching*, 44-46.

[6] Among the silliest things I have ever hear was a statement by a Facebook friend, and cessationist, who said that if a person wears glasses he or she should not be in the healing ministry, because they don't practice what they preach. Ugh! He does not understand "Now, but not yet."

[7]

Carolyn coaching healing prayer at one of our workshops.

Two years ago Carolyn had a car accident. As she turned a corner the early morning sun blinded her and she kept going were there was no road, and off an embankment. One of the doctors who treated her in the hospital told her it was amazing she lived through it, and only fractured her backbone in several places and broke her sternum. She was out of the hospital in a month, and did another month of rehab before she came home. She had to walk with a cane, and her balance is not good yet. Then Carolyn took a bad fall a year ago which broke her femur bone. She has been bed ridden since in spite of many prayers by myself and others. "Now, but not yet."

Even as Carolyn is bedridden we continue to pray for each other. She is in a one-person hospital bed at home, so I can't cuddle up to her as close as we would like. But I do have a cot next to her bed, which I use to take naps or the first part of nighttime sleep. It is really not very comfortable, and when she falls asleep I tip-toe out to the guest room to a bigger bed. To the point, I have had the beginnings of Carpel-tunnel syndrome in my right hand for years, and Carolyn had prayed it to practically disappear. But it has resurfaced recently. As I lay next to her she takes my hand and prays against the Carpel-tunnel syndrome with soaking prayer until she falls asleep. It is subsiding again.

Bill's Journey

I have had a few health issues, none of which have been life threatening. But as a middle aged man I already had a weakness in my right knee. Thirty years ago I first noticed that if I drove a long time with my foot stable on the gas pedal, as in driving on an Interstate, I would get pain in the knee joint. Carolyn would then take over the driving as I transferred to the passenger seat, stretched my leg, and took a Goodies tablet (that particular pain remedy seemed to work best for me). We did not start a prayer routine about this, as it seemed unimportant.

But a dozen years ago I had an arthritis attack in the same joint and was in constant pain and limited in motion. Carolyn and I then began praying for the knee with some regularity. I also learned that alfalfa tablets might help. I tried them and they greatly helped. I was soon walking in complete normality – again, a combination of prayer and supplements.

But occasionally there would be a new, dramatic flair up in that knee. I remember one Sunday I hobbled into church and a young boy in our congregation came up to me and offered to pray for my knee (we trained them right!). He laid hands on my knee and prayed a command prayer and my knee was healed immediately.

Two decades later, at a service in the assisted living facility (noted below), I was preaching energetically and as I turned to demonstrate a point, "snap" went my knee. Horrible pain! I had to finish the service sitting down and then hobbled to the car on one foot with Carolyn assisting me.

I made it to the VA hospital the next day on crutches. The orthopedic doctor showed me the x-ray and said that arthritis had worn down the cartilage on my knee joint. There was nothing that could reverse it. She solemnly added, "This will never be healed. It will only get worse. When the pain gets too bad we will do a knee replacement for you." She gave me a prescription for a strong pain killer, and I was fitted with a knee brace.

For a month Carolyn and I prayed consistently for my knee to be healed. At night in bed as we cuddled she placed her hand on my knee and commanded complete healing in Jesus' name. I began taking alfalfa again with the supplement glucosamine-chondroitin. It is now six years since my knee "event" and I walk completely without pain. Between walking the dog and my duties at work I average about a mile a day. I use a light brace only when I plan walking longer. I take several alfalfa tablets every day as anti-inflammatories.

Two summers ago I had to drive twelve hours straight for a conference I was giving on healing prayer in Illinois. I expected to stop frequently and walk around some and perhaps take a Goodies. I did not have to do either. My knee was in better shape than it was thirty years ago. PTL!

Alas, Ol'Scratch is always up to no good. Recently I twisted my knee again (not preaching this time, but doing some gardening) and again pain and paralysis. But immediately I spoke to and rebuked my knee in the pattern described in Luke 4: 38-39. I said out loud:

> "Look knee, you are known throughout the world from people who read my blog postings, as **miraculously healed.** To be crippled and out of order now would disgrace the name of Jesus and his healing power. Therefore, be healed in Jesus' name! Return to perfect function!"

Wow, within thirty seconds or so the knee stopped hurting and I was walking on it again. I have had no problem since.

About fifteen years ago I needed a miracle on another issue. I mean really, like an "old 'timie," tent-revival, Pentecostal type miracle. Pentecostal evangelists of old used to go around and lay hands on folks with bad dental problems, and sometimes, behold… divine gold fillings. Dr. Francis MacNutt, in his book *Healing*, cited miraculous teeth fillings and healing in the draft of his book *Healing*.[1] The editor thought this was too radical for the charismatic audience of the 1970s who were barely accepting the idea of healing prayer, and suggested it be cut. MacNutt insisted, and the

---

[1] Francis MacNutt, *Healing* (Notre Dame: Ave Maria Press, 1974).

section was placed in the back of the book, allowing the reader some time to get used to the idea that serious miracles do happen.[2]

As for my case, I had gone to my regular dentist two years before and he recommended that two of my wisdom teeth be pulled. But that demanded a dental surgeon and was costly. I let it go without action. But then I began experiencing constant pain in the wisdom tooth areas. I asked my prayer group to pray for a miraculous healing for my wisdom teeth, and they laid hands on my jaw and prayed. So did my wife. She had additional motivation as she knew dental surgery would be a cost put on our credit cards.

In my ministry as Hispanic pastor I had sporadically ministered major teeth healings. It was not a consistent gift, but occurred often enough for me to notice and offer such type of prayer to those who needed it in my congregation.

One case in particular was dramatic. It was a young non-documented Mexican woman with terrible teeth and serious gum infection. The public nurse told her that, unless she had serious dental care, her teeth would all have to be yanked. She came to one of our church's home groups and asked for prayer. I was present as visitor and offered to pray for her. I did so with the usual command prayers, "Gum infection leave in the name of Jesus. Teeth be healed and restored in Jesus' name," etc. but I felt no strong anointing or the flow of the energies of God through my hands as I sometimes do. Nothing happened immediately. But later that night, as the woman was sleeping she was awakened by an "Alka-Selser" type buzzing in her mouth. She went to the bathroom and washed out her mouth and discovered that her gums and teeth were perfectly healed.

With this in mind, when I first started with the problem with the two wisdom teeth I began laying hands on and praying for myself. Often I would drive to work with one hand on the wheel and another on my jaw, praying, "Wisdom teeth, be healed in Jesus name, return to normality!" For a few days the pain would go away and I thought

[2] Personal conversation with Dr. Francis MacNutt, circa 2006.

healing had taken place. But it returned and I went into a new cycle of prayer.

At this time a traveling healing evangelist was doing a healing mission in a town in middle Georgia. He had a reputation for praying for teeth successfully and often gold fillings would appear in the supplicant's mouth where cavities had been. So off I went to one of his meetings, in pain and my hand on my jaw as I drove, repeating, "In Jesus' name, spirit of pain be gone…"

When I got there he immediately greeted me and invited me to share the pulpit and healing line. He had read *Quenching the Spirit* as a seminarian and it had made a great impression on him.[3] In any case, I joined in the ministry and laid hands on several people with good results (no teeth ministry this time). The evangelist then laid hands on my jaw and commanded healing for my situation.

Later that night I drove back home with one hand on my jaw, "Pain be gone in Jesus' name." Nothing had happened. ("Now, but not yet.") But there is a happy ending to this story. One of my Anglo friends at church was a prosperous lawyer with many professional connections. His own dental surgeon, who had pulled out his wisdom teeth, was an Evangelical Christian. He talked with him and the surgeon agreed to pull out my wisdom teeth at no charge from him, but he had to charge for his assistant's wage and the normal clinic fee. My lawyer agreed to pay those costs.

When the dental surgeon examined and x-rayed my mouth he recommended that four of my wisdom teeth be removed, even though only two were in crisis. I asked if that would cost more (to my friend) and he said yes. I asked that only the two teeth in immediate distress be pulled. He warned that in only a few years the other two would be in the same situation and have to come out. I considered, but again asked only two be removed.

The operation went splendidly. When I awoke from it I asked if they had started. He chuckled and said it went very easily. He gave me a strong pain prescription (as normal to the situation) and a small bent syringe to

---

[3] William De Arteaga, *Quenching the Spirit* (Lake Mary: Creation House, 1996).

wash out the holes in my gums as they contracted to fill in the gap where my wisdom teeth had been. That night I took one pain pill and nothing after that. I had a "sensation" in my mouth for some days that I could not call pain, and went about my pastoral work. At the checkup three days later the surgeon was astounded at how quickly the gums had healed and closed. In a dramatic gesture, he took the syringe and threw it over his shoulder, saying, "You don't need this."

My quick recovery really was unusual. A friend of mine, who has scant regard for prayer, had two of his wisdom teeth removed about the same time, and he was in misery for a week in spite of the pain killers. Prayer works even when the miracle you want doesn't happen like you want.

On the issue of miraculous gold fillings, some ask, why in these cases does not God restore and re-enamel the teeth? Sometimes that happens, but very rarely. But I believe there is a reason why more often miraculous fillings occur. It is that our tooth decay is the product of an improper and intemperate diet (i.e. lots of refined sugar). For instance, the skeletons of many ancient peoples, like the ancient Romans, have practically perfect teeth – refined sugar had not been invented. Re-enameling a tooth would have God saying, in effect, "It's OK the way you ate, and go back to eating Twinkies, etc." But with a gold filling God says, "In my mercy, I will do for you what the best dentist would do, but not affirm your eating habits." This is not a direct quote from the Lord. I have not had a specific revelation on this, nor can I quote the Bible on this, since I find no reference to tooth decay in the Bible – no sugar in Bible times. But this is my sense on the spiritual dynamics of this issue – if you have a better take on this please let me know.

I should add that Christians in the healing ministry often need the prayers and help (and medical attention) of others. The gift of healing, like that of the other gifts of the Spirit, such as prophecy, **is normally for others.** Thus normally, a prophet prophesies for others, not himself. Now praying healing prayer for oneself is more common, and I am sure many readers have done that many times. But it is often necessary to have others pray for the situation. For instance, I generally don't post a Facebook prayer request if I catch a cold – Carolyn and I pray through those ourselves. But if we were diagnosed with cancer I would ask (really, pester) all my Christian friends to continuously pray for us. In this I am reminded of the Bakkers, the great healing evangelists and church planters of Mozambique, who had a period of serious illness that needed both the prayers of other Christians and medical attention. Similarly, Agnes Sanford, the great healing apostle of the 20ᵗʰ Century had two bouts with cancer which were healed by the prayers of others and medical procedures.

Lastly let me also say that the ministry of teeth healing is perhaps more in the nature of the gift of miracles than the gift of healing, though both intersect with a "fuzzy" boundary. For instance, healing has normally to do with the energies of God's acceleration of the body's God-given ability to resist disease and heal itself. Physical healing has a natural dimension to it, as even the meanest atheist often recovers from serious disease by getting rest and medical attention.

But if a person lost an arm or a leg, there is no natural bodily process to restore that limb, although some lower order animals can do that feat. If a human limb was restored in prayer, it would not, properly speaking, be a healing, but a miraculous event, and under the "gift of miracles" (1 Cor12: 10).

In this regard I am reminded of one of the great miracles in Agnes Sanford's life. She was serving as a Red Cross volunteer in an Army hospital in WWII when she encountered an infantry officer who had his stomach blown out. He was slowly dying of starvation, as intra-vinous feeding at the time was unable to sustain a person for very long. She laid hands on him and got her telephone network of prayer groups to pray for him. He was miraculously given a new stomach and walked out of the hospital as a born-again believer. This incident is recorded in her autobiography *Sealed Orders*.[4]

---

[4] Agnes Sanford, *Sealed Orders* (Plainfield: Logos International, 1972). I could give you the page number on this but I want you to read the whole work – it is one of the classics of Christian biography.

Judy's Healing

Twenty-five years ago Mike came into Carolyn's counseling office for help. He had recently divorced and was concerned that his children would be harmed by the trauma of parental separation. Carolyn counseled with the children and helped them navigate this difficult period in their lives. About a year later, Mike came in for advice. He had met up with his high-school sweet heart and was interested in marrying her. But burned once, he wanted a Christian and professional appraisal of Judy, the woman in question. Carolyn had her in and found her to be in excellent psychological and spiritual shape, and a great match for Mike.

Mike and Judy married and in fact established a successful marriage. Carolyn and Judy became best friends. But Judy began to have medical problems, and after several doctors' visits was diagnosed with a serious case of scleroderma. This is an ugly and most often fatal auto-immune disease that hardens and distorts the internal organs and the skin, making the latter leathery and hard – an awful diagnosis.

When Judy finally told Carolyn about her situation she was in bad shape, and in dialysis for her failing kidneys. Carolyn and I were at St. Jude's then and we went into high gear for healing prayer on Judy. We visited her at home where a dialysis machine had been set up, and I proceeded to rebuke the disease and anointed her with blessed oil. We did soaking prayer with her on several occasions. To the surprise of the doctors, she improved enough that she could get out of the house and drive by herself.

At the time I led a weekly prayer group at our home, and she became a regular. At each session we laid hands on her and prayed for her healing with command and soaking prayer. We invited her to St. Jude's one Sunday where we did a "communion huddle." That is, Carolyn and I, and a few others took Holy Communion and returned to the pew where we all laid hands on Judy and prayed against the disease.

Judy on the "hot seat" of our home group about 1987.
Note the young man with ample black hair behind her,
anointing her with blessed oil (yours truly).
(Picture is in author's collection)

Mike and Judy were Catholic, and after a month or so of the communion huddles they returned to their Catholic church on Sundays, but Judy continued to come to our weekly prayer group. The scleroderma receded instead of proceeding as would be normal to her case. Medication has also played a hand in her healing, and now, over two decades later she still has to be careful of her diet and continues to take medication.

The disease left her with some distortion on her hands, but her internal organs and skin are OK. The four of us have remained loyal friends and regularly celebrate Christmas and Easter together. Both Mike and Judy have experienced various medical problems, none as serious as the scleroderma, and of course we always pray for each other at the first diagnosis of illness.

We are all "senior citizens" and of the group only I am in better health than her. She enjoys making frequent trips to stay with her daughter and grandchildren who live in North Carolina.

Consistent and timely prayer allowed her to come this far. She is still active in her local church and a food pantry, although very recently Mike's ailments have taken much of her attention. (Now, but not yet).

Our Nov. 11 Vet's get together three years ago:

Judy is on the left with Carolyn,

yours truly in the center with, my buddy Lee and his wife,

Linda, to my left. Mike, Judy's husband, is next to Lee.

Mike saw much combat in Vietnam as a marine.

3

Healing and intercessory prayer at assisted living facilities

Initially Carolyn was skeptical of MacNutt's theory about the difficulty of age related healing prayer (see above). Certainly, the saints and heroes of Pentecostalism were famous for living long and illness free lives. Smith Wigglesworth, the English plumber and healing evangelist cited above, lived to the ripe old age of eighty-eight without illness. Kenneth Hagin, a controversial figure, but a man full of faith and anointed to heal, did not go to a doctor or occupy a hospital bed from his childhood until the week before he died.[1]

But we both came to understand MacNutt's wisdom when we began a ministry at an assisted nursing home. The folks there naturally had all sorts of medical problems, some quite serious. Our ministry had some successes, but less than at our normal church healing missions.

---

[1] Some persons mistakenly assume that if a person's theology is not perfect, he or she cannot be truly used by God. This is nonsense. For instance, Martin Luther the founder of the Reformation and a wonderful re-presenter of the Christian orthodoxy about salvation through faith alone, was a fierce anti-Semite. His anti-Jewish writings were used by the Nazis to help justify their demonic policies towards the Jews. Analogously, most of Kenneth Hagin's theology of faith is very good and useful, but with some exaggerations and errors. I can personally testify to his healing anointing. Several times in the 1970-1980s I stood in his healing line and was instantly healed of various maladies.

Many of the older people had various stages of arthritis and we were able to pray relief for its pain for many of them. Carolyn has always had a gift of praying against pain, and was very helpful in this area. But only a few major healings were accomplished. One woman had Tourette syndrome, which causes involuntary movements and vocalizing. She was healed of this affliction after repeated prayers over many weeks. (Carolyn also has the gift of "divine stubbornness" in prayer.) Another lady with macular degeneration of a very rapid kind had the disease stop after we prayed for her, but it was not reversed. Her doctor was surprised. She died still being able to walk around and see, but not read.

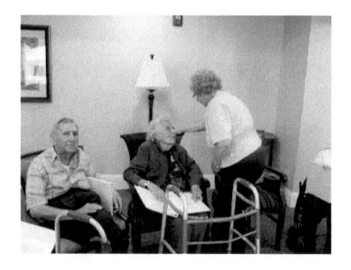

Carolyn praying over one of the people at the
assisted living facility.

We tried several times at praying for the dementia patients in the 'memory wing." It was not successful. Now, I am not saying this as an absolute, and perhaps some person out there will find a successful way of praying against serious dementia and Alzheimer's. I am only saying that MacNutt's insight about the greater difficulty of praying for certain conditions among the aged is *generally* true. It is part of the *"Now, but not yet."*

From Christ the King

The Anglican Church in Hiwassee, Georgia, Christ the King, has a wonderful old age ministry, with seventeen volunteers (and one dog) in active ministry. They minister at two nursing homes and one memory care facility in their area, running weekly worship services and praying for the elderly. Their services include hymn singing, simple preaching and the distribution of Holy Communion. As anyone who has participated or served in these services knows, the elderly, even those suffering from dementia, especially appreciate hymn singing. It seems the area of the brain associated with music is the last to fade – but it could also be that their human spirit, which is intact, can make contact with the handicapped brain through sacred hymns. Something similar happens when those with dementia take Holy Communion; they seem to light up with peace and joy. This is true even if they come from a denomination that gives little emphasis to Holy Communion.

I had the privilege of witnessing several of Christ the King's elderly services, and saw how the volunteers joyfully loved, helped, and prayed for their elderly cares. I asked the volunteers to write down some of their experiences in their ministry. Here are a few of their responses. One of the lead volunteers, George, wrote:

"At one of my very first services a 92-year-old lady wandered in during the sharing of the word. Immediately she got still and tears began flowing down her cheeks. After the service the attendant came over and told me she wanted to talk to me. She held my hand and said:

> I'm 92 years old and I have been backslidden for a long time. When I was a young woman I loved Jesus, attended church and served the Lord. Then I met a man who I fell in love with and married. He wasn't a Christian and he didn't want us to go to church, so we didn't. We had children and raised a beautiful family but I never returned to Church. I heard the beautiful singing and the word of God being spoken and I had to come in and join in. I want to repent of the choices I have made and rededicate my life to Jesus Christ, will you pray with me?

We prayed and she asked me to pray for her family that they would come to know Jesus too."

At another location, another volunteer reported: "In one of the very first services I ever attended, a lady with Alzheimer's came into the service and became very loud and disruptive so I went to her and held her hand and asked to come and sit beside me during the service. That day we all sat in a big circle in a smaller room and as the word of God was shared she became very attentive, but also continued to be loud and disruptive. I took her hand again and called her name and said to her, "Jesus Christ gives you peace" and she quieted down and remained quiet throughout the remainder of the service. She even took the communion willingly and we just continued to love her as she was taken back to her room."

He also recalled: "The cutest little lady who wears her hair in gray braids attends our service each week. (She could be Willie Nelson's sister). When it was time each week for Holy Communion she would say, "No", or would actually leave the room. But during the week before Christmas, I played the carols on the organ louder than usual. There were a good number of residents who attended and who sang along. On that day when we were serving Holy Communion, she nodded her head "Yes" and participated in Holy Communion. I was so happy —I teared up and held her hands and told her she had made my day. She has taken communion ever since. The Holy Spirit must have finally reached her heart."

While visiting the services at Christ the King I saw something I had never seen before. The leader had taken the time to write encouraging scriptures on strips of paper which were individually given to the elderly. The leader of the group recalls:

"We had a new visitor [from the facility] in our church service. She kept talking out loud and was fussing with the other residents. We asked her please listen and not disturb the others. We had written several encouraging Bible verses on stripes of paper and handed them out to the residents. Such as, "God loves you"..."You are a child of God,", etc. When this lady read hers —she calmed down and kept repeating, "God loves me". Her whole countenance changed. God had touched her heart."

Christ the King volunteers
used by permission by Karen Yager

A prayer warrior in assisted living

As our bodies age and we retire from our secular occupation, it is not a time or excuse to be less useful for the Kingdom of God. All to the contrary, our retirement frees up time for Christian volunteer work. Further on, when our bodies get worn out and mostly immobile, opportunities open for ever increasing levels of intercessory prayer.

Let me show this by describing what happened to a person in another assisted living facility from the one Carolyn and I ministered in. She began to practice "praying the news" (described below). She was of course, elderly, and her daughter could no longer meet her medical and caring needs so she was placed in a nice assisted living facility. I knew the woman from thirty years ago when I was a lay person at St. Jude's Episcopal Church in Marietta, then a center of charismatic activity. She was a devout and prayerful person who often volunteered for church service and projects.

But in the nursing home she became deeply depressed. Her daughter called me to visit with her and pray for her. Carolyn and I visited her. I discerned that her depression came from a sense of purposelessness. That is, she felt she now had no further task on earth, and merely had to wait for death to release her to the heavenly realms.

She had a frail body but a perfectly sound mind. So I gave her an assignment to "pray the news," and gave her some instruction on how to do this. I also urged her to pray for the staff and any patients she came into contact with at dinner or recreation room. I urged her to listen to the Holy Spirit for hints on how to pray for those around her, and tasked her to become the prayer warrior of her nursing home. Several weeks after that visit, her daughter called with the wonderful news that her mother was completely transformed. She now loved life and her situation, and was in very high morale as she passed the day in various pray projects, and be- coming the prayer intercessor the Lord had designed her to be.

This is an encouragement for not only those of us who are nearing very old age (I am a young 76) but for those who become disabled or injured and must lead a more retired or inactive life. We can all be prayer warriors to the day we are called to our heavenly home, which will be all the nicer, since we will have spent so much time in prayer.

Praying the news

Now let me say a thing or two about praying the news. This is an intercessory ministry that can have profound repercussion for the good in our local community and nation. It is something that can be practiced by both young and old, but it has special relevance and opportunities to those who are disabled by age, accident or disease and have the luxury of spending consistent time in front of a TV.

The "news" is by its nature, mostly negative. An airliner that makes it to its destination is not news, but one that falls out of the sky is. The story of couple who stays faithfully married and successfully raises four children is not news, but a murder of any one by another is. News agencies have pondered this issue, and there is no good solution. Nice news is dull, as in a company newsletter that feature someone's forty years of loyal service. In the past years national TV networks try to include positive news stories such as "the person of the week" segment on Friday night on CBS, but this hardly stops the bombardment of negative stories.

For many Christians tuning into the news is depressing. Sometimes we just don't listen to it, or turn it off rather than listen to a particularly disturbing item. But this is a wrong response for the mature Christian. We are indeed born into a fallen world, filled with the consequences of corporate and individual sin. So bad news is true news, but also useful as prayer opportunities presented to us.

The Lord has sent us into this planet to bring Him glory and alleviate with prayer, fasting and loving acts the evil and chaos we learn about and encounter. Negative news gives us opportunities to "stand in the gap" for our nation, and for the salvation and welfare of others. The model for this is Moses, when God informed him that He was about to annihilate the Israelites after they had sinned by creating a golden idol while Moses was up on the mountain. What worse news can there be? And what more au- thoritative news anchor man? But Moses interceded, and actually changed God's mind; yes, that is what the scripture says, and the Chosen people lived and were permitted to go on to their destiny. (Exod 32:11-14).

I know of several Christians who have given up on this country or on interceding for it. One has become a survivalist who stocks an arsenal of assault rifles, gold bars, and truck load of freeze dried food to survive a coming war. (Isn't that wonderful Christian eschatology?). The proper Christian course is to trust in God's mercy, and to continue to pray and fast for revival, and for the restoration of America to its Christian roots.

Another pertinent example for intercession is Abraham's intercession for Sodom and Gomorrah. All that God demanded in order to spare those cities were ten righteous men, a small percentage of its population (Gen 18: 22-33). Certainly, praying born-again Christians make up a substantial minority of Americans, certainly more that the ratio of ten to 1,000 or so which would have been the top figure for Sodom and Gomorrah. We must keep praying and trust in God's mercy. We must also keep organizing concerts of prayer for revival, and for corporate repentance for our horrible moral decline. But on the daily basis, we can pray for the healing of our nation as we listen to the news.

Let me give a fictional example of a local murder, varieties of which come across our local news all too often. Tonight at the 7-11 at Main and First two men robbed the store and shot the store manager, Mr. Fred Jones.

Mr. Jones, was pronounced dead on arrival the hospital. He is survived by a wife and two children, ten and twelve years old. Police are on the lookout for the two armed men shown in the store video. If you have any information, please call....

The prayers for such an incident are obvious. Pray for the grieving family, that the Holy Spirit would walk with them through the grief process. Pray that the family would not suffer long term trauma or bitterness, and be provided for. Pray that the police would find proper leads (and avoid false leads) and the criminals would be quickly apprehended without further violence. Pray that they would come to justice and repentance for their crimes.

After some commercials comes the weather girl who stands in front of a weather map and says:This weather front, which brought a foot of snow to the Rockies, is now turning dangerous. We are posting a severe weather warning, including high probabilities of tornadoes for a large section of Kansas and Oklahoma for tonight and tomorrow morning. This is a big storm, capable of generat- ing very large twisters...

Many Christian still do not know that they have every bit as much authority to still storms as Jesus did. He gave us that authority (John 14:12). Further, Christian history is full of accounts of Christian monks and other heroes of the faith ending storms or changing the direction of winds.[2] The pall of cessationism, that disastrous theology that the age of miracles is over, is still the major obstacle for Christians to really take authority and stop the tremendous damage of tornadoes and other storms.

Here are some of the prayers I would say to the threat of tornadoes coming towards us. "In Jesus name, I rebuke this storm and command its energies to be loosed evenly in rain and wind that will not harm people or animals. I ask the Holy Spirit to position and stir up prayer intercessors who know their authority in Christ as watchmen, so that they will com-

---

[2] See my blog posting "Is Calming Tornadoes a Christian Ministry?" *Anglican Pentecostal*, Posted June 1, 2013.
https://anglicalpentecostal.blogspot.com/2013/06/is-calming-tornados-christian-ministry.html

mand any funnel cloud off populated areas and to harmlessly discharge their energies."

If tornadoes have already touched down and the news program is showing the destruction, the prayers would be in this order: "Father, in Jesus name, I pray for angels to support and sustain persons trapped and injured. I pray for the emergency responders to be led supernaturally to the survivors without delay." And, "I pray for wisdom and divine coordination between all the government and volunteer agencies involved in this rescue effort."

Let me note that the classic work on interceding against destructive storms and natural events is the book by Mrs. Agnes Sanford, Creation Waits, which is still in print.[3]

The national news comes on. After a run down on the political situation, which lately is very disturbing, a video comes on of a bombed out section of Baghdad, with ambulances, medics working, and bodies lying on the ground. The news anchor declares, "An ISIS suicide bomber detonated a truck bomb in a busy food market yesterday, and at least twenty-five are dead and another hundred wounded, many women and children."

Our "flesh" mind, ably assisted by Ol' Scratch, might lead us to thoughts such as, "Hey, Muslims killing each other again. Great, let them finish each other off."

No.

We need to pray for the victims of such attacks just as we would for our own tornado victims. In these Muslim on Muslim incidents I always add prayers for the conversion of the Muslim peoples. That is, the majority of Muslims in these terrorist afflicted countries are aghast and depressed over these violent acts, and feel utterly helpless to stop them. I pray that they will "connect the dots" and understand that the Koran itself is the problem. I pray they come to understand and accept that there is another book which is really God's word of mercy and love. I have blogged on how to specifically pray for the Islamic peoples, including composing prayer psalms for them, and how to support the many satellite ministries that are bringing about an amazing harvest of Muslim conversions.[4]

---

[3] Sanford, *Creation Waits*. (Plainfield: Logos International, 1978).

[4] I have done several blog postings on this topic. One is "Praying for the Conversion

Let me suggest that pastors try an experiment. Encourage three or four families to get together at a home for a pot luck dinner, but instead of Bible study that night, listen to the news, local and national, and then "pray the news." See if this type of prayer event catches on. (I get very frustrated that I am a retired pastor, and can't try this stuff out in my own congregation before I suggest it to others.)

Imagine what would happen if just 20% of Americans practiced praying the news daily, or if churches all over America had these "praying the news" potlucks once a week.

More to our topic on assisted living facilities, what if church volunteers organized some of the patient and occupants of an assisted living and nursing home to gather together and listen to the local evening news and pray the news in the ways suggested. Might not this both give them a motivation for continued life as useful empowered intercessors, and would it not bless the local community? I would wager that if this were done by multiple churches and assisted living communities in a certain town or city, the police in that city would gain the reputation of being crack investigators and crime stoppers.

of the Islamic Peoples." *Anglican Pentecostal*, Posted Dec. 16, 2014. https://anglicalpentecostal.blogspot.com/2014/12/a-call-to-prayer-let-church-be-what-it.html

4

Spiritual direction and transformation at old age

[From 2010–2015, a friend of mine had the opportunity to "Elder Sit" with older persons in their last years. Susan Brooks Thomas is a Spirit-filled Prayer Warrior with a deep interest in healing and spiritual well-being. I will let her explain one experience in her own words.]

Over the past decade, I have had the opportunity to minister to beautiful people well aware of their imminent transitions from this earth. Some of whom have already moved on.

I found that as many of us age, we harbor deep seated bitterness masquerading as disappointment and resentment as our bodies begin to shut down and hitherto main-stream activities are curtailed. Whether we withdraw intentionally or are forced to the sidelines, we generally don't like being put out of action.

Three of our greatest dilemmas—loneliness, fear, and uncertainty—sometimes disguise deeper issues such as unresolved or unrecognized bitterness, unforgiveness, and deceptions about the Person of God. These are tough to admit as we assuredly think that by now we have it all together.

Many of us are retired from highly successful careers in the business world, some have been dedicated Church members for many decades, perhaps others are retired from demanding service professions. We have "been there" and "done that" and believe we have overcome our issues, faults and/or sins. Self-examination of our inner Spirit-life is not something we anticipate at this stage. Believers know where we're going, and

45

the non-believers try to rest on their own goodness, karma or contributions to society. We are the generation that thrives on do-it-yourself, independence, and pride in being "open-minded." Therapy, drugs, self-help programs, and conferences have prepared us for our golden years. Right?

A few years ago, I was asked to meet with a lady who had been housebound for years due to several aliments that limited her mobility, and had serious susceptibilities to infection. She had been unable to attend worship services for more than a decade, but often hosted a few people at a Bible study in her home.

She reached the point where she was unable to clean her small mother-in-law apartment, much less have the vigor to prepare for the studies. One of her closest friends, still welcomed to visit her, asked if I would come in weekly to dust and Swiffer her home.

When I arrived, her daughter-in-law met me on the front porch and asked me to remove my shoes and coat and run a clothes brush over my jeans and sweater to remove any potential dander or pollen before entering. No problem.

I was then requested to move a straight-backed, non-upholstered chair from the dining area to sit in for my interview. Janey was a very bitter, ill-tempered woman in her mid to late 80's, with bright intelligent eyes proclaiming she was still mentally sharp. The actual interview consisted of itemizing the duties expected and laying down strict house rules.

Janey showed me her stop watch. I was expected to be punctual, would be paid a dollar amount well below minimum wage (non-negotiable), was to bring my own water, but not any kind of food or snack, and would not be allowed to refill my water bottle from her tap. She preferred I did not use her toilet and most importantly, she was not interested in any social conversations. And of course, since I have pets, I must keep separate clothes in her garage to change into before I entered her house.

While she was talking, my heart broke for the internal pain which propelled her to be so controlling. Accepting that this was a ministry opportunity rather than a route to a healthier bank account, I agreed to everything. Now, I am a tall, sturdy, well-padded woman and Janey was nervous that I would be the "bull-in-a-china-shop" with all of her collections of lighthouses, angel statues, and a myriad of other knick-knacks that would need weekly dusting. She wanted me to leave her a cash deposit to cover anything I might break. Firstly, I did not have the cash amount she wanted and secondly, my educated, sophisticated pride bristled at the assumption I would be a clumsy oaf. Before I could refuse, however, her daughter-in-law entered the conversation and dissuaded Janey. While her daughter-in-law was speaking, the Holy Spirit informed me that I had to get over *my* attitude and that He would then develop this as to be a ministry point for Janey.

After two weeks of watching her laboriously figure out my check amount to the dollars and cents, passing my trial period and understanding the work involved and the time, I offered to come at the specified time once a week, clean the kitchen after she had prepared and finished her lunch, and be finished by an agreed-upon time, for a flat rate of $25. I put it in terms of being for my budgeting convenience.

Watching her hard glistening eyes widen and soften slightly at my suggestion was my first reward.

I prayed constantly while there. My prayers concerned her physical condition certainly, but my main focus was her inner pain. Occasionally, I was led by the Holy Spirit to discretely anoint her bed, favorite chair and refrigerator.

This awkward relationship continued through the rest of the summer. By Thanksgiving, she would respond to my greetings and conversational farewells. The approaching holidays gave me openings to discuss her plans and learn a bit more about her family situation. Our mutual friend had shared (with Holy Spirit prompting when she realized I was in this for the long haul) about Janey's long, bitter marriage to an abusive law-enforcement officer in another state. And about her children that seemed to only need her substantial bank account.

One of the tenants of secular psychology and an underlying premise for the plethora of self-help books and gurus that continue to flourish in this age, is the focus on individual worth and self-love. Unfortunately, these concepts become quite distorted, leaving out the concept of sin and leading to a cultural obsession with cataloging wrongs perpetuated against ourselves, either intentional or perceived. This spirit of offense is anti-Biblical:

> A person's wisdom yields patience; it is to one's glory to overlook an offense. (Proverbs 19:11)

And the seeking for and retaining of lists of slights was actually addressed by Paul in his marvelous passage describing Love and what the believer should aspire to

> It does not dishonor others, it is not self-seeking, it is not easily angered, it keeps no record of wrongs. (1 Corinthians 13:5)

Janey and I developed a relationship during the Christmas season that allowed us to talk about many things, especially Scripture. However, I was not there to listen to her repeat and re-live all the abuses from her itemized list, nor was I there to support her perceived identity as a Holy Martyr for having endured them. And while her declaration of forgiveness for her ex-husband was not mine to examine, we did mention the cleansing aspects of God's Love, exchanging bitterness for a higher understanding.

> Above all, love each other deeply, because love covers over a multitude of sins. (1 Peter 4:8)

There was agitated denial that we needed to work on issues of control, fear and ego/self-importance with its roots in pride and bitterness. These issues needed to be lined up with Scripture and overcome. This was not a popular concept, and her flesh and friends certainly let me know. Janey's inventory of offsetting good points was presented. She had raised three children under that abuse. She had also worked outside the home, saved and invested wisely, she bought a house for her son (The one with the guest cottage next door where she lived), she had established another son in a business and she supported her daughter as a single mom. She had provided funds for them all to go to college, and there were gifts of boats and cars, etc. So of course she was a very loving person.

On the spiritual front, she hosted a Bible study in her home, and gave generously to her church and many ministries. In fact, she hired me. All wonderful activities and her friends and family took great pride in her.

But there was a miserable old woman hiding behind a reputation of being a faithful, loving person. Janey did not realize she reveled in her "sufferings" with the self-righteous attitude she was holy because of them. She believed she was entitled to the accolades and could use them as a weird type of currency. In the misleading way of a lot of us, she was mistaking pride for dignity and Godly love.

Unfortunately, Janey's family turned away from God because while they enjoyed and demanded the material benefits, they also saw her for what she was, a very sick, likely dying, very controlling, and shriveled woman. There were no longer any demonstrations of the peace and grace she preached. That was a god they wanted no part of and the more Janey tried to strong-arm them to accept salvation, the faster they ran.

I choose this woman as the focus for this chapter as she embodies an affliction affecting many believers, but is generally not apparent until we reach a point where we have time on our hands, are incapacitated in some way or have a crisis. Then we must examine where the secular world has tricked us and intruded into our Godly life. This is generally not fun and our flesh rises up with the rebel cry "This isn't fair." "I don't deserve this, look at all I do for you, God," "Why are you doing this to me?" or the worst one—and we women are real good at this type of manipulation—"I will just be strong (in myself) and suffer this and ignore you, God, until you come to your senses."

And we thought that rotten apple was no longer an issue.

That great underlying sin –pride rears its head here. Handling a slighted pride, not to be confused with dignity, requires a good long raw look in our mirror. And at my age, that is not always a pretty sight. Especially if we are looking at our flesh. Surely, just as we examine our bodies for abnormalities, we must also learn to recognize self-righteousness disguised as virtue. I think it is important to cleanse our spirit-selves at all times from the bitterroot and unforgiveness and to recognize a prideful heart. And to give God the fear of living without these thoughts, attitudes.

This is a very deep seated condition, an unaddressed darkness cleverly hidden in some of our souls, especially Janey's.

By New Year's, while she was ambulatory, her health had deteriorated. My weekly visits had become mostly a time of ministry with the peripheral activities of cleaning Janey's house, preparing lunch and doing laundry.

She was still upset because I wasn't interested in her litany of stuff that had happened to her over the years and caused her to act like she did. "It was only natural" I heard her say, nor would I validate her standing as a victim. However, we do not, indeed, cannot, earn salvation or God's Love or His Kingdom by good works. At one point she became very exasperated with me and yelled, "But I have earned the right to act like I do!"

Janey admitted that she wanted to just give up because she was having a hard time accepting that her last years were not what she had planned. She herself now struggled to believe and trust a supernatural Creator, a Father who loved her. She was indeed looking forward to her new life as a Bride of Christ, but no linger believed in His very real and living presence while she waited. After all, He disappointed her and did not applaud all she had accomplished for Him in her earthly life.

That realization opened a way to explore selfish and false concepts of forgiveness. She had exchanged her persecution for a subtle, but vicious pride. Essentially she clung to a "see-how-good-and-strong-I-am-because-I-could-forgive-stuff-like-that" attitude. I don't think that is the humility God means.

> For by the grace of God given to me I say to everyone of you not to think more highly of himself and of his importance and ability than he ought to think; (Romans 12:3a AMP)

As Janey's physical and family situation worsened, she became increasingly angry with God for allowing it. This dear woman had set herself up in artificial high place and now waffled between thoughts that she was good enough to have God do as she wished, and swinging to the other extreme of despair or guilt. Even worse was believing the lie that she was bad enough to have drawn all the crisis to her. This guilt, unresolved or false guilt, is a favorite weapon of Satan.

Like many of us, Janey knew and confessed that God was with her in all her trials, albeit sometimes as a vague and distant goodwill. But God was calling her to realize that she failed to understand that it is not our own strength and worthiness, or that any of us deserve Him, but it is God's very nature to reside with His people. How often our own selves get in the way and prevent us from seeing and often from receiving all the good He has for us. What a beautiful blessing He was offering her.

Through speaking the Truth in love, prayer and searching Scriptures, Janey realized the truth of her relationship with God's goodness and undeserved grace. The Holy Spirit exposed the bitter roots of incorrect thinking. We articulated a diagnosis, and were ready to accept the cure.

For a while, we had been closing our time together with prayers. We now added specific prayers and praises including prayers for Holy Spirit indwelling and enlightenment. Janey allowed me to lay hands on her and pray in the Spirit, speaking in tongues.

As a Bible study leader, Janey had studied and was well versed in some Scriptures. What she knew, she knew very well, however she had limited knowledge of the entire length and breadth and depth of God's Word. She knew only the verses she taught, as she herself had been taught in a cessationist church. With the Holy Spirit's help, we began to search out unfamiliar passages, especially those about pride, bitterroot and the glories of God's personality. We spent much time reading and praying verses revealing the truth of forgiveness and depth of agape love God pours out on us. Regardless of our self-worth or accomplishments. We change. God doesn't.

I loved watching Janey mature as she completely internalized the beauty of Grace. Her healing was in accepting that it is not ours, not hers, not mine, but it is our Sovereign Father's unconditional mercies and Love. He reaches for us. His Love, His Forgiveness, His mercies and His provision, are going to cover us regardless of our sin or strength of faith or accomplishments. Forever. Beginning right now as soon as we ask.

Janey dusted off (or rather I dusted it off for her) her old Concordance and with a fresh hunger devoured God's Words. She studied the Ten Commandments, every verse about His Kingdom. She feasted on His promises and spent hours basking in His presence. Her daughter-in-law told me that where before there had always been a gloomy silence surrounding the cottage, music now spilled from the open windows. After-all, there is no demon, dis-ease, germ, bacteria, virus, darkness or distorted idol that can stand in the presence of the Living Lord.

Every week, brought a glorious change in Janey's countenance and her behaviors. She was pleasant, cordial and glowed with that love-light we all have when we spend time with God. Her physical health continued to decline, but she no longer cataloged each problem. When it became time to hire a full-time nurse, Janey was a non-stop witness, in words and personality, to God's salvation. She read Scriptures out-loud as long as she could and when her voice was tired, asked the nurses to read them to her. That was interesting as many of the care-givers were not believers when they arrived. She stopped trying to force her opinions on her family and in curiosity, they began to question her about the change they saw.

The Hospice Chaplin was a very nice, sweet, caring pastor, but she came from a cessationist denomination and wasn't Biblically sound. Janey set about to enlighten her. Janey planted acres of Holy Spirit Truth seeds in this woman, and while it has taken years and much watering by others, I have seen God's growth in her ministry.

Shortly after Easter, Janey fell and was admitted to the hospital. Our mutual friend and I drove down to visit. While everyone was saying she could return to her cottage in a few weeks, we knew better, but it was OK. While we visited, the light in her clear eyes was brilliant. She was so full of joy, peace and love; attributes that had long been missing in her life. She asked us to pray and the Shekinah glory was almost overwhelming. We were laughing and crying and celebrating, much to the chagrin of some hospital staff, but for once understood the meaning of the old term "Homecoming, Going Home." Her eternal home. When the tearful call came a couple of mornings later from her son, my spirit leapt in joy, for this dear sister was now physically reunited with Her Glorious Bridegroom –Jesus Christ.

> "No temptation has overtaken you except what is common to mankind. And God is faithful; he will not let you be tempted beyond what you can bear. But when you are tempted, he will also provide a way out so that you can endure it." 1 Corinthians 10:1

Father, please forgive us when we want to think it all us. It is not who or what we are or have accomplished. It is all about you, Who you are, what Jesus accomplished on the cross and the utter audacity of

Your Love and Forgiveness.

Forgive us when we are tempted to let fear, guilt, care & worry become idols.

Please give us the courage to live this new life, humble, loved, forgiven and fill us with your resurrection power as we break off the deadly bounds of lies.

Thank you for your right & Holy Spirit to enlighten, sustain, encourage & guide us!

© Susan Brooks Thomas
3/5/19 Kilmarnock, VA

5

Healing the elderly via long distance prayers

Now let me discuss a form of prayer that has special relevance to the elderly, long distance healing prayer, especially via phone. Long distance prayer can also be done as a special form of intercession using Holy Communion as its vehicle.[1]

Agnes Sanford used the Holy Communion form of prayer as her first inner healing prayer (c. 1946). The case was of Jewish American war veteran, Harry Goldsmith, whom she had ministered to and converted while he was recovering from a serious combat wound. After his physical recovery he was still seriously afflicted by the memories of the torment and abuse he experienced as a young Jewish boy in Nazi occupied Czechoslovakia. He escaped from Europe because his mother was an American citizen, and right after the U.S. entry into World War II, diplomates arranged an exchange of American civilians in Nazi occupied Europe for German citizens stranded in America.

But for Harry the veteran, trivial events would sometimes make Harry break out in an irrational rage. Agnes tried praying for him in various ways to alleviate this, but to no effect. Then Agnes learned of a Catholic Medieval technique from nearby Anglican nuns of praying and fasting for someone in distress, and taking that person's griefs, burdens and hurts

---

[1] This section is modified from my earlier blog posting, "Spirit to Spirit Healing," *Anglican Pentecostal,* Posted Aug. 15, 2018. https://anglicalpentecostal.blogspot.com/2018/08/spirit-to-spirit-healing.html

to Holy Communion (based on Gal 6:2). To be clear, this was a spiritual action, without the physical laying on of hands of normal healing prayer.

Agnes covenanted with the Lord to take on Harry's sorrows and hurts from his childhood. She prayed and fasted for him for a full week. She could tell her spirit was making contact with Harry's spirit because she began experiencing some of his emotions of hurt, rejection and anger that had no relation to her life situation. On Sunday she went to Holly Communion on behalf of Harry, and she was relieved of those alien emotions at the same time that Harry was healed of them. Harry did not even know Agnes was interceding for him, but he suspected she had done something, and called her to find out. I give a full description of this case in my book, *Agnes Sanford and Her Companions.*[2]

Agnes saw this type of intersession as human spirit to human spirit (with the assistance of the Holy Spirit). The human spirit of the intercessor made intimate contact with the spirit of the needful person. Later, Agnes learned that the long period of prayers and fasting was really not neces-

---

[2] De Arteaga, *Agnes Sanford*, Chapter 17, "Harry and the Healing of Memories."

sary. What was essential was taking the person's hurts and distress to Holy Communion. Agnes warned that using the prayer and fasting technique in its original form could open the intercessor to demonic spirits if this is attempted with a non-Christian, where demonic entities may reside.

Carolyn and I have done the abbreviated form of spirit to spirit intercession over the years, some very successful, others not so (healing is a mystery in any mode that you pray). In any case, I was intrigued by this form of spirit to spirit healing and intercession, and I ventured into and tested something I have not seen in the literature of healing (1 Thess 5:21).

As background, I normally use the "Hunter method" of arm and leg extension, etc., for physical healing (described above). This method is especially effective in back problems and pain control. Several years ago I used the Hunter method via the telephone to contact a needful person, and prayed by using words and my imagination and asking the supplicant to do the same. The person had, in this instance, a back issue but could still stand. I asked her to stand and interact with me as if I were right there. I told her to extend her arms in front, and I would do the same, as if we were touching arms, even though we were at a far physical distance. I then commanded in the name of Jesus, the extension of the short arm.

It may never be known who was the first to do the Hunter method via telephone. God knows. I learned of it 20 years back from a person in my Hispanic congregation shortly after I taught a class on the Hunter method. The lady, Rosa, had a special anointing for healing and had an aunt in California who was in severe pain, so she called and talked her through, in a very detailed manner, about the arm, pelvis and leg extensions, as she commanded the healing. I actually did not repeat what Rosa had done for over a decade until I was forced to do so in the case cited above.

I have now done these telephone healings at least a half dozen time in the last few years, mostly with excellent effect. And last year I tried a variety of it that I had never done before. The person who called for help was bedridden and unable to even put her arms out fully. All she could do was tap her cell phone on. I asked her to put it on speaker and follow my instructions. I told her to shut her eyes and in her *imagination* see herself standing and responding to my instructions. First, to extend her arms in front, as I imagined I was in front of her touching her arms. Over the telephone I then commanded her arms to equalize, in Jesus' name. Similarly, I did the "pelvic thing" via our imagination. She felt immediate relief from the pain she was suffering even though she was in bed, and had not physically moved her body. I do not know how much recovery she experienced, and if she ever walked again, but she experienced very substantial pain relief that she had not experienced before even though some Christians had prayed for her.[3]

I believe the best explanation of her healing was that it was a spirit to spirit communication of the power of the Holy Spirit and the name of Jesus to heal. That is, by faith and through our imaginations her healing went to her spirit and cascaded down to her body.

What happens in these long-distance healing might be termed "spiritual entanglement," which has a parallel in the science of quantum physics called "quantum entanglement." That is, the property of certain particles to interact instantly regardless of space between them, yes even faster than the speed of light.[4] For instance, if an atom is bombarded by certain particles, and particles from of the atom are thrown out and go in opposite directions they may be "entangled." This means that whatever happens to one of these particles happens to the other instantly, even if they have traveled in opposite directions for light years. Einstein, who helped develop the mathematics of quantum physics, could not believe that anything could communicate faster that the speed of light, even though the equations he developed said so. He died not believing them, and hoping that someone would correct them to greater accuracy – and away from entanglement. But in fact, entanglement is true and has been experimentally verified.[5]

---

[3] I suspect much of the praying for her was done by prayer groups who pray over a list of names, "Lord, heal Sussi Jones of her heart condition," etc. This sometimes works, but is generally ineffective.

[4] I explain this with more detail in both *Quenching the Spirit* and *Agnes Sanford* in chapters on spirituality and quantum physics.

[5] Michelle Starr, "Physicists prove Einstein's "Spooky" quantum entanglement," *C/Net*. Posted, Nov. 19, 2015. https://www.cnet.com/news/physicists-prove-einsteins-spooky-quantum-entanglement/

Paul talked about our spiritual entanglement as Christians in these terms:

> Is not the cup of thanksgiving for which we give thanks a participation in the blood of Christ? And is not the bread that we break a participation in the body of Christ? Because there is one loaf, we, who are many, are one body, for we all share the one loaf. (1 Cor 10:16-17)

Note also the lengthy description that Paul gives about the Body of Christ in 1 Cor 12: 21-31, as having various parts, but they "entangle" to the point that, "If one part suffers, every part suffers with it; if one part is honored, every part rejoices with it." (v. 26)

It seems that the universe was created with the entanglement characteristic from the beginning and at its base to enable sacramental activity. Of course, this characteristic is also used by the Demonic realm, as in Voodoo dolls, etc., using the spiritual energies of the Kingdom of Satan.

But to our main point, and regardless of whether this explanation is true, close to the truth or not,[6] Christians not only have the authority and power to pray for healing at a distance, but can use the very effective forms developed by the Hunters for physical healing without having to physically touch the other person.

Note that like Carolyn's healing of her kidneys and her non-entrance into dialysis, my lack of a need for knee replacement surgery has saved a lot of medical insurance money, not to mention deductibles and personal bother. Insurance executives note well! The discussions and deadlock about modifying or repealing "Obama Care" has a core problem. It is that modern health care, with all its devices and modern medications, has become immensely expensive. The auxiliary issue it that we have an interest driven medical establishment in America which will not accept reasonable

---

[6] I use the phrase "closer to the truth" often in my writings, reflecting the philosophical insights of one of the greatest philosopher of the 20th C., Karl R. Popper. In his study of the history of science and how it progresses he discovered that no theory of proven to be absolutely true, but it may be better than other theories. This type of humility would do the discipline of theology much good. See Karl R. Popper, *Conjectures and Refutations: The Growth of Scientific Knowledge.* New York: Harper & Row, 1968.

solutions to reduce the cost of health care. Europe does much better, but that is another issue.

But what would happen if healing prayer was taught to volunteers at a given company? They would then be known as persons of healing prayer to be sourced by the other employees when a medical situation arose. Would days absent from illness and medical claims go down? I think so. I did a blog on this very issue but have had no offers to test it.[7]

---

[7] William De Arteaga, "Can Teaching Healing Prayer to Company Employees bring Down the Cost of Health Care?" *Anglican Pentecostal*, Posted Jan. 20, 2015. https://anglicalpentecostal.blogspot.com/2015/01/can-teaching-healing-prayer-to-company.html

6

Countering a Heart Attack

In this chapter I wish to give the reader guidelines on how to pray for a person experiencing a heart attack. As we age, and our friends age with us (what an amazing coincidence!) we are more likely to find ourselves in a place where a heart attack is happening.

First, let me begin by recounting an incident that happened to Carolyn and me about thirty years ago. It occurred shortly after Carolyn and I had completed a course on the Hunter's method of command prayer. Carolyn and I were at her son's wedding in Baltimore. He had invited his favorite professor from his college days to attend. When the elderly gentlemen got near the church he began having chest pains and he sat down at a brick ledge just to the side of the church. As Carolyn and I approached someone had called 911 and a policeman was already there. The policeman was in communication with the ambulance on his radio. As he monitored the professor's vital signs he said to the ambulance medic, "Hurry up, he needs help right now."

Carolyn and I immediately started to pray for the professor. Carolyn prayed in tongues, and I paced back and forth, a few feet from the scene, praying aloud, but not shouting, "I rebuke the spirit of death from this place. I speak to the heart, and command you to be well, repaired and restored in Jesus' name." Carolyn varied between tongues and command prayer. We continued in that vein for several minutes.

The policeman again said on the radio in an irritated voice, "If you guys don't get here in a few minutes, he's gone." (The dialogue is approximate, this happened 30 years ago, but not exaggerated in any way.)

Carolyn and I continued praying and commanding healing in Jesus' name. I placed my hand on the professor's shoulder and continued praying out loud. The man was unconscious and it did not occur to me to ask the policeman for permission to lay hands on the person for prayer. He knew we were praying, and seemed to appreciate the fact. When the ambulance finally showed up, it had been delayed by a traffic accident along the route, we prayed for wisdom for the medics and the doctors at the hospital.

Then we went in to the service which proceeded with just a brief delay. Most of the participants did not know about the drama that had just occurred at the side of the church. Several hours later at the reception Michael got word from his professor that he was doing well. The blood work showed he had a major heart attack, but his heart was beating strong and normally, as if he had not had one. PTL! (This account is found in Carolyn's book, *Watching God Work:* If there are slight variations in the vocabulary and description, well, it is just like the synoptic Gospels!)[1]

Several years ago, as I was putting the finishing touches, *Agnes Sanford and her Companions,* I reread Mrs. Sanford's classic, *The Healing Light (1947).* I had forgotten that there she described the healing of a person dying from a heart attack. It gives a wonderful account of Mrs. Sanford's "combined" healing technique of gentle command healing, graced visualization, mental prayer, and the laying on of hands.

The incident occurred about 1945. Mr. Williams, her next door neighbor, was a cessationist and did not believe in healing prayer. He suffered from rheumatic fever and had a damaged and weak heart. One night he returned from work at point of death, and his children rushed over and begged Agnes to come and pray. She found Mr. Williams slumped on a chair in living room, his heart beating furiously and erratically. She went over:

As soon as my hands were firmly on his heart, I felt quiet, serene, in con-

---

[1] De Arteaga, *Watching,* 51-53.

trol. Forgetting the heart, I fixed my mind on the presence of Our Lord and invited Him to enter and use me. Then, Mr. Williams being quite unconscious, I talked informally to his heart, assuring it quietly that the power of God was at this moment re-creating it and it need labor no longer. Finally, I pictured the heart perfect, blessings it continuously in the name of the Lord and giving thanks that it was being recreated in perfection. Soon I could feel the hearts beats becoming more quiet and regular. I could even feel that strange inner shifting that reports the rebuilding of flesh and tissue."[2]

When the doctors next examined him they were astounded that it had gone from grossly swollen to normal size and rhythm. Now of course, my actions and Mrs. Sanford's were not identical, but let me offer some guidelines:

1. Take authority over "spirit of death" and banish it from the immediate presence.

2. Begin praying by speaking to (commanding) the heart to be healed and recreated to its normal design (I use the words, "To the pattern of Jesus Christ.")

3. If the person is conscious, ask permission to lay hands, preferably close to the heart, and pray that energies of God pass through you and completely heal and repair the heart. This may be done as a visualization as you continue to command the heart to respond to the healing grace/energies from the Lord.

4. As you pray, give thanks to God that the healing is being accomplished.

5. Pray for wisdom and effectiveness in the arriving emergency responders and medical attendants.

Lastly, I am reminded that the standard Red Cross First Aid course includes actions taken for a heart attack victim. Of course calling 911 is the first step. This is followed by chest compressions and infused breathing, which most person are now familiar with. How would these actions

---

[2] Sanford. *Healing Light*, 96.

be combined with healing/command prayer, especially if there is only you and the heart attack victim in the room? I would do the prayers after I made a quick call to 911 and *as* I was doing the chest compressions? I have not had the opportunity to try it. Perhaps, "one, two, three, "heart be healed in Jesus' name"… six, seven eight, "spirit of death be gone"… The key element is to do all that is medically possible while concurrently inserting prayer.

7

Aging gracefully for old dogs and other animals

A few months ago a nurse visited Carolyn, now bedbound, to check on her progress. As she was filling out some forms she glanced over at our dog Sasha, and stared at her for a moment or two. Then she looked at me and asked, "How old is your dog?" I answered, "Thirteen or fourteen. We are not sure."

She then said, "I think your dog has a heart or lung problem, her breathing is not right." The nurse is not a veterinarian, but has had several dogs, and with her medical training has been able to diagnose dog problems effectively. I told her "Thank you, I'll attend to it." She probably thought I would take her to the vet. Actually, Sasha had an exam a few months earlier and was declared in good shape, and not due for another exam for some time.

But I had noticed that lately Sasha was reluctant to follow me upstairs, something she normally did when I went to my desk or take a nap in the guest room. This was different from just months ago, when she followed every time I went.

I did in fact attend to Sasha's problem with healing prayer. In the evening when I came from work she would greet me and follow me to my favorite chair. There I would spent some time petting her. Now I would also place my hands on her chest and command healing in Jesus's name. Since I did not know the exact name of the illness, I would say, "Spirit of infirmity leave Sasha!" and then declare her lungs and heart perfectly normal. After doing this several nights I noticed Sasha was no longer reluctant to follow me upstairs. Healing had taken place.

Three years ago we had an earlier incident of illness and healing with Sasha. Carolyn, who is more sensitive to animals than I am, noticed that Sasha was walking with a limp. I looked but could see nothing, but in fact noticed that mid-way through our normal walk the she began to limp. So I took her to the vet. Sure enough the vet diagnosed arthritis on her pelvis area, as common to her age and breed. She recommended doggie joint medicine, glucosamine-chondroitin, just like the human kind.

I shared with the vet that I had taken that for my arthritis in combination with alfalfa tablets and with prayer, and was healed completely (story of my knee, above). She said she believed in the effectiveness of prayer and also mentioned that she had heard of alfalfa used on dogs, but she had never prescribed it. She excused herself to do internet search on this and within five minutes came back and said that indeed alfalfa was recommended for doggie arthritis. But she did not find anything on dosage. I shared that I took three tablets per day, and given my weight and Sasha'a weight, one tablet a day would seem right.

I began a regimen of adding the laying on of hands to our usual petting time. At night I would give her alfalfa and half of a tablet of glucosamine-chondroitin from my medicine cabinet in peanut butter. Within two weeks she was walking perfectly normally.

Actually, Sashas's first healing came without either Carolyn or myself consciously praying for her. She came to us as a one-year-old, and had been malnourished as a puppy. When she first came to us she ravenously ate everything that was edible (and some things that were not). We had to be careful how we stored food and closed cabinets, etc. I asked my friend Doug, a dog expert, if Sasha would grow out of this, as we fed her regularly and plentifully. He said, "No, the dog is imprinted in the starvation mode, and will be like that till the day she dies." We were OK with that, as Sasha was a very loving and intelligent dog.

Early on Sasha and I developed a routine for my "off from work" days. In the morning Sasha would come to my "prayer closet" (actually, a swivel chair in my study) and nuzzle my arm to get my attention. I patted her, gave her a treat, and did a quick prayer for her. Usually it was something like, "Lord, give Sasha every doggie blessing she can contain." I lay hands on her head, and went on with my other prayers as she went off to munch on her treat.

About four years ago we noticed a real change in Sasha's behavior. She did not seem as perpetually hungry, and at time left her bowl of food unfinished. We usually give her table scraps, but now we noticed she was picky as to what she ate. For instance, she no longer wolfed down leftover Salmon skin or carrots. All of this points to a healing, even though we did not specifically pray for it. It seems that God freed her of her starvation imprinting as part of the "doggie blessing" I prayed for.

I should have prayed for her in a more focused manner, the way Carolyn and I did for "Tuppance," a Boston Terrier we had when we were first married. (see just below) Why it did not occur to either Carolyn or myself to pray a specific inner healing prayer for Sasha I cannot explain. Perhaps the Lord wanted to show us the healing benefit of blessings our animals.

Inner healing for animals, old or young

Does inner-healing prayer truly mediate an energy and grace from the Lord, or is it no different from imagery conditioning practiced by humanistic psychologists? This was an issue debated a decade ago when inner healing first became popular. Those involved in the inner-healing ministry have felt the frustration of trying to explain that positive results from their prayers are not just the product of suggestion.

To be clear for those not familiar with the inner-healing ministry, it is a form of healing prayer that developed out of Agnes Sanford's healing of Harry (discussed above). In its most popular form, a counselor leads the supplicant through a meditation in which he or she recalls a difficult or traumatic experience, but now invites Jesus into that memory. Marvelous healings happen as Jesus intervenes in the memory and the supplicant often experiences positive emotional and behavioral changes.[1]

---

[1] For a discussion of how inner healing changed from a Holy Communion intercession, to suggested imagery see my discussion in *Agnes Sanford,* chapter 17.

The late Dave Hunt and others had raised the question of inner-healing as a form of psychological manipulation and witchcraft.[2] But even before their criticisms were made, the evidence of inner healing as a grace was difficult to discern. In the typical counseling situation there are multiple factors in play, such as the counselor's loving attitude and counselee's expectancy and openness to suggestion. It is easy to claim that the healing and behavioral changes experienced by the supplicant were the product of suggestion working with his or her expectations.

The issue of inner healing as grace or gimmick is similar to that of how to discern the grace of prayer for physical problems. Many times, illness is treated by both prayer and medical interventions; and an attempt to attribute the precise degree of effectiveness to prayer, as against surgery, medication, and so on, is at best problematic.

Some of these complications can be short-circuited when we examine what happens as we pray with animals for inner healing. Animals can be injured emotionally; these injuries can cause them to behave and react badly. But animals are not able to accept suggestions that would change their behavior immediately.[3]

Agnes Sanford practiced both healing prayer for physical ills and inner-healing prayer for animals. Naturally, the overwhelming bulk of her efforts were dedicated to human needs, and the times she ministered to animals were few. These healings were mentioned mostly in her talks at church missions and Camps Farthest Out (a nationwide network of summer retreat programs). Mrs. Sanford believed that animals are easier to heal than many humans because their minds offer no theological or philosophical objections to the possibility. They are not capable of belief or

---

[2] For instance: Dave Hunt and T.A McMahon, *The Seduction of Christianity* (Eugene: Harvest House, 1985); Don Matzat, *Inner Healing, Deliverance or Deception?* (Eugene: Harvest House, 1987).

[3] Just how much animals can understand is the subject of ongoing research. Dolphins certainly can respond to simple symbolic commands, as in: "Place Frisbee in basket." However, no evidence exists for the capability of animals to respond to suggestions of a healing nature. The complexity involved in associating mental imagery with behavioral outcomes is far too great. See Susan Chollar's, "Our Cognitive Cousins: Conversations with the Dolphins," *Psychology Today* (April 1989), 52-57.

unbelief, as far as we know, so the faith necessary for the healing must come from the human prayer intercessor.

The first account of Mrs. Sanford's ministry with animals is found in one of her juvenile novels, *A Pasture for Peterkin*.[4] Mrs. Sanford called her novels "teaching parables," and, like others she wrote, this one was loosely based on events in her life. In this case, the setting was her summer cottage in rural Massachusetts.

In the novel, Amanda, age nine, prays for her sick and dying calf, Peterkin, with the laying on of hands and by visualizing the animal as happy and well. Amanda realizes that the calf cannot help in the healing prayer: "I know you haven't the sense enough to believe it, and God knows it too, so I am going to believe it for you."[5] After the prayer, the calf recovers and grows to be a happy bull with its own pasture.

A factual description of the inner healing of an animal came only in Mrs. Sanford's last major theological work, *Creation Waits* (1979).[6] Here, Mrs. Sanford described an inner healing ministered by her secretary and traveling companion, Edith Drury. Mrs. Sanford was in Devon, England speaking on healing. A local farmer asked for prayers for "Sheila," who lately had been "nervous and upset." Mrs. Sanford, assuming the Sheila was his wife or sister, sent Edith to minister. When Edith arrived at the farm, however, she discovered that Sheila was the farmer's cow.

Edith honored the farmer's request anyway, praying:

> "...that the love and light of God would go all the way back through Shelia's heifer-hood, healing all traumatic experiences, remembered or not, in her subconscious, and make her a happy, cream-filled Christian cow, certainly with no more tendencies to kick and be nervous."[7]

The prayer worked, and the cow was healed of her emotional and behavioral problems.

In the course of our own ministry a dramatic inner healing came about thirty years ago for our Boston Terrier, Tuppance. Once, just before a thun-

---

[4] Agnes Sanford, *A Pasture for Peterkin* (St. Paul: MacAlester Park, 1956) 36-37.
[5] Ibid.
[6] Sanford, *Creation Waits*.
[7] Ibid., 113

derstorm, Carolyn let Tuppance out in the back yard to piddle. As she neared her favorite spot by a large oak, the tree was struck by lightning. Carolyn, standing at the back door and twenty feet away, felt the shock and was thrown backwards. Tuppance was less than a foot from the tree. The concussion threw Tuppance to the ground, and she ran, terrified, into the house.

Thereafter, any explosive sound would send her into panic. Well before we could hear an approaching thunderstorm, she would begin pacing, breathing rapidly, and drooling. If the storm took place at night, she would jump on our bed and continue her panicky behavior. Fourth of July was a nightmare for the dog. Tuppance's anxiety continued for a year.

This happened in 1981, while I was researching the history of inner healing and was reading all of the works of Agnes Sanford. I suggested to Carolyn that we pray for the dog. I led the prayer, but there was no appreciable change in Tuppance's response to thunder. We tried again later, and this time Carolyn, who has always had a special compassion and love for animals, led the prayer. She held the dog and prayed simply: "Lord Jesus, please find that little dog that was so frightened by the storm and comfort and heal her."

After Carolyn's prayer, there was a dramatic change in Tuppance's behavior. Thunderstorms no longer put the dog in panic. She would come to one of us for "company," but there was no more rapid breathing, drooling, and pacing. We could peacefully sleep through a summer thunderstorm, with Tuppance *under* our bed, not on top of us. She died several years later of old age and a weak heart, but never again showed exaggerated behavior to loud noises.

This little canine case history (and the other accounts of animal inner healing) have some profound implications. The mind of an animal cannot take complex symbolic suggestions.[8] Behavior modification might have worked on Tuppance with a skilled and patient trainer: for instance, the setting off firecrackers followed by rewards. But this was not the case.

---

[8] H.F. Harlow, "The Formation of Learning Sets," *Psychology Review* 56 (1949), 51-65, and "Mice, Monkeys, Men and Motives," *Psychology Review* 60 (1953), 23-32.

Major and permanent behavioral changes took place immediately after Carolyn's prayer.

Many pet owners longingly and compassionately hold their pets without reported behavioral-healing results, as we did with our dog. Therapeutic touch is beneficial, but of small effect in comparison to the healing Tuppance experienced. Thus, the important factors in this case seemed to be the inner-healing prayer itself, and Carolyn's special compassion, which focused that prayer.

Let me share another of Carolyn's doggie inner healings that happened just several years ago. We were on a healing mission at a church in North Carolina.[9] Our host, the rector of the church, had a dog called Marius, which he got as a "rescue dog." She was mistreated as a puppy and had constant nightly nightmares. When we learned about that, Carolyn went into action and prayed for the dog's inner healing. No more nightmares.

But beware, if you pray for an animal in a similar manner what happened to Carolyn the next day (pictured below) may happen to you:

We understand that these cases are little more than "anecdotal evidence" – almost a dirty word in behavioral disciplines. However, it would be quite possible to design a veterinary protocol for emotionally injured animals to test this type of healing prayer quantitatively. The results of a well-defined and well-administered test might be a substantial addition to the mounting experimental evidence on the reality and effectiveness of inner-healing prayer.

---

[9] It was a marvelously successful mission, recorded in my blog posting: "Church of the Redeemer – healing Workshop." Posted Oct. 27, 2015. https://anglicalpentecostal.blogspot.com/2015/10/church-of-redeemer-healing-workshop.html

Sweet Pea

Sweet Pea was a plain gray cat, and at the time of the incident we describe, old, but still spry. We don't remember how she arrived at our house. The problem for the cat was that the next-door neighbor's house sat less than a stone's throw away. Sweet Pea received lots of petting from the teenage daughter, but cars, zoomed in and out of their driveway.

One afternoon as Carolyn got out of her car after work, out of the corner of my eye she saw Sweet Pea sitting on top of the woodpile on the side of our house. She often perched there keeping an eye for the chipmunks that lived underneath, so she didn't really think much about it. After dinner, Carolyn put down her dish by the refrigerator and called Sweet Pea. She didn't appear which was unusual when food was involved. She went looking around the yard.

Carolyn found her in the same spot on top of the woodpile. But something just didn't seem right. Sweet Pea didn't respond, other than to look at her, even when she called, "dinner," a word she understood perfectly. Carolyn walked back inside and called me. "There's something wrong with Sweet Pea." When I looked at her, I said, "I think she's sick. Let's pray for her." We put our hands on her back and we prayed. We talked to God about any rotten rodent she may have eaten, any infection, or any kind of infirmity. As an afterthought, Carolyn prayed, "I come against any pain for this little cat."

Sweet Pea didn't resist or complain when I lifted her up and took her in the house. She didn't move, but just sat on the sofa where Carolyn pet her, but she showed no interest even in her favorite shredded turkey dinner. Before bed Carolyn put her hand on Sweet Pea again and prayed against infirmity and pain. In the morning Sweet Pea still sat in the same place, not paying attention to food nor wanting to go outside. "I'm going to take her to the vet," Carolyn said.

I drove and Carolyn held Sweet Pea on her lap, praying all the way. She didn't seem in any discomfort, but didn't seem right either. Certainly Sweet Pea was sick. The doctor said after examining her, "I think she may have an injury. Let's get some x-rays." An assistant took my cat to x-ray. Within a minute or two she was back with a stricken look on her face. "I'm so sorry," she said, "but your cat died on the x-ray table." "I need to see her," Carolyn said, heading for the door. In the x-ray room she held Sweet Pea and cried. "I'm so sorry," she said to my cat as she took her in her arms.

The doctor disappeared and returned with the x-rays. "I can't believe this," he said. "Almost every bone in her body was broken. She must have been run over. She must have been in excruciating pain, but I didn't see any signs that she was in discomfort."

God didn't heal Sweet Pea, but did He take away her pain as we prayed.

8

Dying Gracefully

Lee Buck: Life lived well, and death with heavenly dignity.[1]

One of the problems of Pentecostal and charismatic folks is that often don't know or discern when it is time to die. I have heard several of them say, "There is no New Testament model of a funeral, except to raise the dead!" or some foolishness like that. An incident happened when I was assisting priest at Light of Christ, my home congregation which illustrates this sad fact.

One of the founders, and vestryman (elder) of our church Light of Christ Anglican Church was Mr. Lee Buck. A wonderfully godly man. He was born into extremely poor circumstances, raised by his mother during the Great Depression who barely had enough money to feed him and his brother. Lee recalled that in primary school his clothing was so worn out that the teacher sent him to a local Civil Conservation Corps station where classes on sowing were taught to the unemployed. One of the students was tasked to make Lee a set of clothing. It clothed him, but was so ill fitting that when he returned to his class he was laughed at by the whole class.

---

[1] Attending the dying has not been my specialty. But I asked my clergy friends what books on the Christian way of dying they would recommend, and these came up. The classic of the genre is Jeremy Taylor's *Holy Living and Holy Dying* (1650 and 1651), available on the web as a free download. Several modern works were highly recommended, Donna Authers' *A Sacred Walk* (Charlottesville: A & A, 2014) and the most recent award winning work by Matthew Levering, *Dying and the Virtues* (Eerdmans, 2018).

It was a traumatic experience and he vowed that he would not be poor as an adult.

Lee got hold of a used saxophone and taught himself to play. So well in fact that as a young man he made a good living from local night spots and was able to support his mother. World War II came and he joined the Navy. He saw considerable combat in the Pacific as an antiaircraft gunner, one of the more dangerous jobs on ship-board, as anti-aircraft guns are in the open and not shielded by armor.

By the end of the War he had earned a commission, and then sent to naval school to learn the technical skill of moth-balling ships into the reserve fleet. During the Korean War he was recalled to take ships out of mothball. Lee went to college under the GI Bill and ultimately earned an advanced degree in history. But, he chose a career in business (professors don't make much money) and rose to become a very successful business executive for New York Life.

Lee had married while in the Navy, and with his wife Audrey raised four lovely girls who now all serve the Lord. The Bucks also took time and effort to foster care for fifteen other children and they did a wonderful job at that.

Lee and Audrey first joined a Methodist church where they both contributed to church life, but without firm belief or enthusiasm. (Most Americans did that as an obligation in the 1950s.) Providentially he was relocated to the New York office and settled in Connecticut, a train ride commute to his office. At that time Audrey received the Baptism of the Holy Spirit at a Bible study. She prudently hid that from Lee, but suggested they attend the nearby Episcopal Church, St. Paul's in Darrien.

The Bucks settled into the Episcopal Church in Darrien. That Church experienced a great Spirit-filled revival in the 1960s under the leadership of the Rev. Terry Fullam.[2] After a period of initial suspicion, Lee was baptized in the Spirit and transited form a nominal Episcopalian into a born-again, Spirit-filled enthusiast for the Lord. He devoured the literature of the Charismatic Renewal and the splendid teachings of the Rev. Fullam.

---

[2] Bob Slosser, *Miracle in Darien* (Logos International: 1979).

Lee had cultivated a gift for public speaking as an insurance executive, and now discovered he has the spiritual gift of evangelization. He combined the two in the heady years of the early Charismatic Renewal (early 1970s) and became a frequent speaker at Full Gospel Bunsiness Means Fellowship (FGBMFI) and other charismatic meetings.[3] In obedience to the Lord's prompting, Lee chose early retirement from New York Life to dedicate his full time efforts to the Lord. This was at considerable cost to his retirement pay – a blow to his quest for material fortune. Lee became a traveling lay elder of the Charismatic Renewal, going all over the world to encourage others to become born-again and Spirit-filled.

I met Lee and Audrey at St. Jude's' Episcopal Church, Marietta, Georgia, in the 1980s where they had moved shortly after his retirement. Although many Episcopal churches were undergoing revival, it was also a time when the denomination as a whole, like many other mainline denominations, was sliding into Biblical disobedience and heresy. Thankfully, St. Jude's remained solidly orthodox and charismatic under its pastor, the Rev. Frank Baltz. At St. Jude's Lee led in organizing multiple charismatic workshops and conferences which influenced many in the greater Atlanta area. He personally brought in such distinguished speakers as Dennis and Rita Bennett, and Dr. Vinson Synan, the dean of Pentecostal historians (and an excellent speaker and teacher to boot).

The drift of the Episcopal Church into heresy became a torrent in the 1980s and 1990s.[4] When Gene Robinson, an open and practicing homosexual was ordained Bishop in 2003 it was the last straw for many of us. Lee and several other lay leaders of St. Jude's decided to separate from the Episcopal Church. That was a painful decision that was repeated in many parishes across the nation.

Lee was one of the key persons in ensuring a smooth separation from St. Jude's to form Light of Christ *Anglican* Church. About half the congre-

---

[3] Sam Justice, "Witnessing With Confidence," *Charisma* (March 1984, 38-41).

[4] The cause was the continuous apostate liberal theology that gripped the seminaries from the 1900s, and was filling pulpits with ministers who did not believe in the miracles of the Bible nor the essential doctrines of the Church. See chapter 23, "The Villains of the Story: The Seminaries as Sanhedrin," in my work *Agnes Sanford*.

gation left including some of the Hispanics who came with me to form San Lazaro, under the wing of Light of Christ.

In 1983 Lee had his first heart attack, and typically he led five members of the hospital staff to the Lord while he was under their care. We prayed for him regularly, but he needed a pace maker implanted, and that went well. By the turn of the new century he had constant problems in his heart – it was simply wearing out and he was forced to slow down. Various medical regimes were tries, but he continued to weaken. In 2006 Lee began to experience jolts from his pacemaker to reset his heart's failing electrical system. Each time it was a painful experience. Then the jolts became constant, two or three a day. This was definitely wearing him out and the pain was awful.

He went to the hospital to see if something more could be done. Several members of the congregation visited and one prophesied over him that he would recover and have "five more years" of fruitful life. I sensed that was wrong and went to visit him. At his bedside we reminisced for a while, and he described the pain the shocks caused him. I told him, "Maybe it's you time to go to be with the Lord. You don't have to hold on if you don't want to. You've lived a long and wonderful life. I am sure the Lord will greet you with, "Well done good and faithful servant." (Matt 25:21). He said, "Thank you Bill, you're the first one to say that. I'll pray about it." A prudent man, he had long made sure his will, insurance and other matters were in order. He had already planned details for his funeral.[5]

The doctors said nothing more could be done for him, and Lee prayed with Audrey about his situation. A few days later he called in his family, daughters, sons-in -laws and grandchildren, and shut off his pace maker. His heart began to slow down, and he passed on to the Lord's presence with his wife holding his hand (September 2006). His funeral was a glorious earthly celebration of a Christian life well lived – but I would wager not nearly as glorious as his reception in heaven.

It was his time.

---

[5] Note that the Lord cares that you leave the earth well, without mess about inheritance, etc. See 2 Kings 20:1

Living for the Lord, but dying in a mess

Our friend Joan' was spiritually prepared for her death, but unlike Lee Buck she did not take sufficient concern to place her material house in order. She was my Sunday School teacher at San Lazaro, and although she never learned Spanish, the children loved her and she did that job faithfully for us. In fact, she would volunteer for practically anything that needed to be done in the church. She was a woman of prayer.

As a young woman, Joan had a successful career as an interior decorator. One of her accounts was with Rich's Department Stores, the high end department store in the Atlanta region. But a decade before she died she lost most of her accounts. She could not use the new computer CAD programs which allowed the customer to see furniture in "virtual reality" and with different fabrics, etc. She worked at other, less lucrative jobs.

Her son got in trouble financially, from poor decisions, and she took out a second mortgage to bail him out. Her last years were spent on the edge of poverty, with a modest Social Security income, on food stamps, and a few odd jobs. She lived in a modest two-bedroom house.

In the last three years of her life she battled cancer. At first, the radiation treatments did very well, and the cancer disappeared. But in a later check-up two suspicious spots appeared on the x-ray. Again she went in for treatments, this round was especially strong and left her exhausted.

Carolyn had lost her counseling office at our church over an incident that was no fault of hers. And as a temporary measure she rented Joan's living room three times a week for her ministry. Carolyn would always bring Joan lunch, chatted with her and prayed with her for her healing.

One morning Carolyn came, but Joan did not answer the door. She went in and saw Joan seated at her favorite stuffed chair, seemingly asleep. Carolyn ate her lunch, then went to awaken Joan. She did not awake. Carolyn called Joan's best friend from church, Lea, and a lady gifted in prayer and prophecy, and then 911. The para-medics were in in just a few minutes. Joan was dead, and had probably died the night before – her blood was puddling in her legs and feet.

As Lea rushed to Joan's house she asked the Lord what was happening.

The Lord told her clearly, "I took her home."

"Is there anything I can do?" she asked.

Lea heard again, "I took her home!"[6]

Lea had a vision of Joan as a beautiful young woman now dancing before the Lord.

After she died our church contacted her son in Texas and he came down for a few days. Carolyn and I helped him sort out her house, and he took a car load of her things back to Texas. Joan was a "collector" and it was quite a job. The most distressing thing was that her guest room was so full of stuff that one could not walk into it. Most of it was sample fabric catalogues from her professional days. These things are large, about two feet long, and eight to ten inches deep. There must have been a hundred of them in the room, dating back perhaps thirty years or more. She never threw out a single one. Her basement was full of older furniture, some of it good, with a few really nice pieces that did not fit into the upstairs, including a really beautiful Wurlitzer piano that needed minor repair.

The worst thing about this is that Joan really had a spirit of hospitality, but she could not exercise it because she had no guest room to share with others. With all the conferences our church sponsored she missed plenty of opportunities.

Three months after we helped clean out the worst of the stuff, including all of the catalogues, I received a call from her neighbor. All her furniture and belongings were out on the street, in the rain. Her house had foreclosed. Her son had not paid the mortgage nor removed the rest of her belongings. The beautiful Wurlitzer sat in mud, and was ultimately junked with the rest of her stuff. That piano could have graced some room in most churches, adult Sunday school room, or youth room, etc.

Now, in the grand scheme of things, all that did not matter much. Joan, I am sure, did not miss a single step in her dance before the Lord. She had, on the important issues of love, charity and service been a "Good and

---

[6] Koontz De Arteaga, *Watching*, 77.

faithful servant," and had entered into her reward. But she could have done better in placing her stuff into the hands of others.

The foreclosure of her home made an impression on me. I was at that age where a sudden heart attack was possible. My father died at sixty-two from one, and I was then seventy. Many of us have trouble giving up our stuff, even when it is no longer of use to us. The industry of rented storage garages thrives on just that issue. The Lord had dealt with me about letting go of certain ambitions and projects that I will not likely complete.

Ten years ago, when I resigned from San Lazaro, I had the ambition of starting a new church that would be bi-lingual and experiment in do-ing church as mandated in 1 Cor 14.[7] But at 76 years old now, and with an over-supply of young Anglican priests in America, that does not seem likely.[8] I have a peace about the fact that my ministry will be writing and teaching, not pastoring. I have already given away several items I saved from San Lazaro, as in a portable podium.

I am also in the process of giving away certain sections of my library. For instance, I had a collection of books by or on Charles Williams. He was a friend of CS Lewis, and member of the Inklings. His theology was profound, and at one point I thought of writing about him. But I discerned I was not called to do that, and gave my collection to an Anglican monas-tery. Similarly, I gave away my substantial library of Spanish literature to a Christian college Spanish professor to give away to her students.

The great example of this getting rid of excess stuff is John Wesley, the founder of Methodism. During his lifetime his books sold widely and he could have accumulated a vast fortune and a big home with attached library. Had you been a pioneer in the American frontier you would have probably had two book, the Bible and his book on herbal remedies.[9] In

---

[7] See my blog posting "Can church be done as Paul Mandated in 1 Cor 14?" *Anglican Pentecostal*, Posted Mar. 25, 2013. https://anglicalpentecostal.blogspot.com/2013/03/can-church-be-done-as-paul-mandated-in.html. To Roman Catholics, having an over-supply of priest does not make sense. That luxury is the product of having the Biblical understanding that priests can be married and be effective ministers (1 Tim 3:4).

[8] John Wesley, *A Primitive Physic: An Easy and Natural Method of Curing Most Diseases* (London, 1760). Modern editions available.

[9] MacNutt, *Healing* (Ave Maria, 1974).

any case, he gave most of his money and possession away, and when he died his net worth was less than £100.

So one of the principals of "holy dying" is to put your house in order, including releasing excess baggage before it is thrown out by relative who doesn't care, or worse, fought over. I can imagine one of my relatives rummaging through my house after I die and saying "Who would want all these old books? Out to the dumpster!" Really, I know an Anglican priest who did that to his rector's library that was in a storage cubicle. I managed to salvage many of those books and have been distributing them to churches in need.

Our generation has an added problem in giving away much of its stuff. The millennials no longer value many of the fine things that were considered worthy of collection and preservation. My wife assembled a collection of fine china cups for years. No one in the family is interested, and their value keeps dropping. We keep looking for someone who would value them for their beauty.

Last word

A friend and devote Christian read the first draft of this book and said, "You're giving too much space to medical and herbal remedies. This confuses the reader. Was the healing a product of God's miraculous healing power, or because of some herb like alfalfa and the other things you mention?" I thought about his comment, and although I appreciate sincere criticism, I believe he was sincerely wrong. Some healing books are indeed written as if medications and medical attention is unimportant, but that in itself is unscriptural. I pointed that out in chapter one that God designed nature with plants that are wonderfully beneficial to us. To downplay the latter is to disrespect God's creative genius and fail to praise Him for it. I keep on taking alfalfa, and when the weather gets rainy, and I feel a tinge of arthritis, I double the daily dose and thank God that alfalfa is not just for cows.

Suggested Readings

Healing Prayer

Bosworth, F. F. *Christ the Healer.* Grand Rapids: Fleming H. Revell, 1996. First published in the 1900s.

De Arteaga, William. *Agnes Sanford and Her Companions: The Assault on Cessationism and the Coming of the Charismatic Renewal.* Eugene: Wiph & Stock, 2015. Historical study.

Hunter, Charles, and Francis Hunter: *How to Heal the Sick.* Kingswood: Hunter Ministries, 1981.

_____. *Handbook for Healing.* Whitaker House, 1987.

MacNutt, Francis. *Deliverance From Evil Spirits.* Bloomington: Chosen, 1995.

_____. *Healing.* Notre Dame: Ave Maria, 1974.

_____.*The Prayer That Heals: Praying for Healing in the Family* Notre Dame: Ave Maria, 1984

Sandford, John, and Paula Sanford. *The Transformation of the Inner Man.* Plainview: Bridge-   Logos, 1982.

Sanford, Agnes. *The Healing Light.* St. Paul: MacAlester Park, 1947.

Intercessory Prayer

Hayford, Jack. *The Secrets of Interce ssory Prayer: Unleashing God's Power in the Lives of Those You Love.* Bloomington: Chosen Books, 2009.

Murry, Andrew. *The Ministry of Intercessory Prayer.* Bethany House, 2003. Originally published, 1897.

Sheets, Dutch. *Intercessory Prayer: How God Use Your Prayers to Move Heaven and Earth.* Bloomington: Bethany House, 1996.

Holy Dying

Authers, Donna. *A Sacred Walk.* Charlottesville: A & A, 2014.

Levering, Matthew. *Dying and the Virtues*. Grand Rapids: Eerdmans, 2018.

Jeremy Taylor's *Holy Living and Holy Dying* (1650 and 1651), available on the web free.

Appendix

Faith Fatigue? A curious case

Healing prayer does not always succeed, "Now, not yet." Sometimes God heals an unbeliever who stumbles into a prayer meeting half drunk, and then stumbles out and never comes back to church or gives God the glory. Remember, that once Jesus healed ten lepers, but only one came back to thank him and give glory to God.

On the other hand, I and everyone else in the healing ministry, if they are honest, have seen very dedicated and mature Christian with serious healing needs that do not receive any sort of miraculous healing. The popular evangelist Jonnie Ericson Tada, who suffered a catastrophic accident which left her a quadriplegic is an example of this. But in her case we can begin to discern why God withheld His healing hand. She has been a tremendous model and encourager to others who have similar difficult circumstance. Other cases may not be as clear.

Dr. Francis Macnutt, wrote a chapter on this issue in his classic work, *Healing*, "13 reasons why people are not healed."[1] Everyone in the healing ministry should read that chapter. The reasons he included are, lack of faith to receive the healing, improper type of healing prayer, as for instance praying for physical healing when a person really needs deliverance prayer first, and other reasons.

Let me add one more category to MacNutt's list: I call it "faith fatigue." I saw this in a nun that I know and have prayed for several times. She is well known in the Catholic Charismatic Renewal and has had a marvelous

---

[1] MacNutt, *Healing*, Chapter 7, "Eleven reasons why people are not healed."

teaching and preaching ministry. She also has had for many years horrendous migraine headaches that often force her out of ministry for days at a time. No medication seems to help.

She has been prayed over by myself and others countless times, and by now avoids receiving any sort of healing prayer. I surmise that the problem is one of being disappointed countless times. I can see her years ago, when the Charismatic Renewal first broke out going to several prayer groups, and encountering persons in the healing ministry, perhaps even Dr. Mac-Nutt prayed over her and nothing happened. Now all she has is a negative faith, that she will never receive healing and must suffer the migraines as some sort of sharing the suffering of Christ. (Rm 8:17) I don't believe that is true in her case, but have not been able to help her or understand her case. If anyone out there has had similar cases, and has managed to break through with healing, please let me know through my Facebook page.

CPSIA information can be obtained
at www.ICGtesting.com
Printed in the USA
LVHW020834240523
747800LV00017B/1405